Carey Martell

Encyclopedia of Legendary Artifacts

The History of
Mythical, Mystical
and Peculiar Items
From A-Z

No part of this publication may be reproduced, or stored in a retrieval system, or transmitted in any form or by any means, electronic, mechanical, photocopying, recording, or otherwise, without written permission from the author.

Encyclopedia of Legendary Artifacts
First Edition, 2015
All rights reserved.
Published by Martell Books
http://martellbooks.com/

ISBN-13:
978-1522831525

ISBN-10:
1522831525

Printed in the United States of America

About the Author

Carey Martell is the Chief Executive Officer of Martell Broadcasting Systems, Inc.

Carey formerly served as the Vice President of Thunder TV, the internet television division of Thunder Digital Media. In the past he has also been the Director of Alumni Membership for Tech Ranch Austin. Prior to his role at MBS, Inc. and his career as a video game developer and journalist, Carey served in the US Army for 5 years, including one tour of duty during Operation Iraqi Freedom. Carey is a member of the Veterans of Foreign Wars.

Carey also moonlights as the host of The RPG Fanatic Show, an internet television show which has accumulated over 3.7 million views.

His blog can be found at http://careymartell.com/

Foreword

Even during the romantic days of Spain, belief in magical items was widespread. No duel or tournament could take place without a formal declaration from the combatants that they carried no relic, engano, amulet or other protective charm that would grant them an unfair advantage over their opponents.

Despite modern science and all the technological advances it has brought us, even today you can find specialty shops that sell charms and trinkets, or purchase books that have detailed instructions on how to craft your own. It seems the human fascination with the paranormal will never go away.

Yet the study of legendary, mythical or magical objects is much more than superstition. The study of mythology is heavily intertwined with the history of human culture. Take King Arthur's mythical sword Excalibur as an example: it has inspired more than just stories, but even a popular Las Vegas casino. Another example can be found in the rod of Hermes, Caduceus, which has become the universally recognized symbol for doctors.

Many people today live their lives unknowingly surrounded by symbols that date back hundreds, or even thousands of years. The symbolism these objects represent have become an integral part of human culture, and puts us in connection with the ideas of our ancestors.

This encyclopedia contains entries for numerous objects that appeared in legends, myths and stories that shaped human culture around the world. Some of these objects were entirely fictional, but some of these objects actually existed (and may still exist in museums) and were used by real people.

In writing about these items I have made little attempt to separate fact from fiction, and have not made any attempt to prove or disprove whether an item and the story behind it was "real" or not. To me, whether they are truly magical or not is irrelevant; these items are legendary for simply being an important part of our history.

And who knows; perhaps these items—or the idea behind them—will have a powerful impact on the shaping our future?

I hope you enjoy reading this book as much as I enjoyed creating it.

Carey Martell
June 4th, 2009

A

<u>Aaron, Ring of</u>: A diamond ring that, according to ancient Hebrew legend, was owned by the grand pontiff Aaron. The diamond was said to shine bright and pure when a Hebrew was innocent of criminal charges, but would become black when they were to be punished for their sins. If the diamond turned blood red before the accused, it meant execution by the sword.

Sources:
 '*Encyclopaedia of Superstitions, Folklore and the Occult Sciences, Vol. II*', by Cora Linn Daniels and C.M. Stevans, J.H. Yewdale and Sons Co. (1903)

<u>Adamant:</u> A mythical material from which many legendary items are claimed to be constructed from.

Adamant and similar words are used to refer to any especially hard substance, whether composed of diamond, some other gemstone, or some type of metal. Both adamant and diamond derive from the Greek word αδαμαστος (adamastos), meaning "untameable". Adamantite and adamantium (a metallic name derived from the Neo-Latin ending -ium) are also common variants.

<u>Adelring</u>: Featured in the Danish ballad '*Sivord and Brynhild*', Adelring is the sword of Sivord Sharensved which his brother Haagan borrows to kill him with. In the song, Adelring is the only sword which can kill Sivord. It is worth pointing out that Sivord Sharensved is seemingly based on Sigurd, and Haagan is based on King Gunnar.

Adelring appears in other tales;

In the Scandinavian song '*King Diderik and the Lion's Fight with the Dragon*', Adelring is a sword that King Diderick finds in a dragon-lair and then uses to kill the dragon which appears in the story.

*"It was Sir King Diderk,
in the hill he searched around;
Then, helped by the Lord, the famous sword
Called Adelring he found."*

In another Danish poem, '*Svipdagsmal*', the sword is given to the main character Svendal by his dead mother, who comes to him as a ghost bearing the gift,

*"I shall give you a good Sword,
That they call Adelring:
You will never come to Strife,
You shall win sure victory."*

In both tales, the sword seems to either be based on the 'Nagelring' of Dietrich of Bern or the 'Naegeling' of Beowulf. (*See 'Nagelring'*)

Source:

'Tragica', Mette Gjoe (1657)
'Edda Saemundar', Sophus Bugge (1867)

Adder: A sword owned by Egill Skalla-grimsson, the hero of the Icelandic tale Egill's Saga, otherwise known as Egla by scholars. The sword is called 'Naður' in some tales.

"He hadin his hand his sword Adder.
Forward Egil pressed, and hewed on either handof him, felling manymen".
Egill wielded Adder with another sword, Dragvendil. Whereas Dragvendil was a heirloom sword which Egill inherited from his father Skalla-Grimr, Adder was won in combat when Egill defeated

Source:
'The Story of Egil Skallagrimsson: An Icelandic Family History of the Ninth and Tenth Centuries', Rev. W.C. Green
'The Epic Hero', Dean A. Miller

Agneyastra: The fire weapon of the Hindu god of fire, Agni. The word Agneyastra is of Sansrkit origin, meaning "fire missile" or "fire arrow". The weapon appears in the stories *'Mahabharata'*, *'Ramayana'*, and *'Visnu-Purana'*. The weapon was given by the wise man Aurva to King Sagara. Agneyastra was said to have been built of 'seven elements'.

Sources:
Mahabharata'
'Ramayana'
'Visnu-Purana'

Agnus Dei: Translated as "The Lamb of God", this is a medieval talisman from the Roman Catholic tradition. The Agnus Dei is made from a cake of wax that has been stamped with the figure of a lamb supporting a banner of a cross. The cake was consecreated by the Pope and supposed to possess such great virtue that it was a safeguard against evil spirits.

Sources:
'Encyclopaedia of Superstitions, Folklore and the Occult Sciences, Vol. II', by Cora Linn Daniels and C.M. Stevans, J.H. Yewdale and Sons Co. (1903)

Alius and Olius: Twin swords that appear in the *'Saga of Asmund Champion Killer'*. They were forged by Aliues and Olious, dwarven smiths from the netherworld of Hel, for King Bundli of Sweden.

Aliues claimed that his sword would shatter Olius if they were wielded against each other, but otherwise they were equal. The King decided to test this for himself and indeed Olius was was shattered, and the dwarf was asked to forge another sword.

However, Olious (who was upset that his last sword was broken despite the warning) placed a curse upon this new sword so that it would someday kill the son of one of Bundli's daughters.

The tale surrounding the two swords bears striking resemblences to the stories concerning Tyfring.

Alius is eventually wielded by Hildibrand, son of King Bundi's daughter Hild and her husband Helgi. The cursed Olius ends up being wielded by Asmundar, his younger half-brother.

As Olious had predicted, the two brothers become compelled to fight one another in a feud over property and marriage, Asmundar kills Hildibrand with Olius.

Source:
'Six Old Icelandic Sagas' by W. Byant, translated by Gudmundur Eringsson
University Press of America 1993 ISBN: 0-8191-9156-6

<u>Almace</u>: (Almice, Almacia, Dalmuce, Aigredure, Autemise, Hautemise) In the French *'chansons de geste'* (songs of heroic deeds) tales, Almace was the sword of Archbishop Turpin of Reims, used by him at the battle of Roncevalles. It was forged from 'brown steel', or 'burnished steel'.

Turpin is injured in the battle by being pierced by four spears, but he continues to fight and manages to deliver one thousand more blows before he dies.

"He's drawn Almace, whose steel was brown and rough,
Through the great press a thousand times he's struck."
(*'The Song of Roland'*)

In the Norse *'Karlamagnus Saga'*, the sword was obtained from Malakin of Ivin, a Jewish moneylender who brought three swords with him that he claimed were forged by Galant (Wieland) the Smith in ancient times so that Charlemagne would release his brother. Malakin had received them from King Faber.

The other two swords were Kurt (Curtana) and Dyrumdali(Durandel) which in this, Charlemagne kept for himself. Kurt was given to Oddgeir and Turpin was given Almacia (Almace).

Sources:
'Song of Roland', translation by Charles Scott Moncrief (London, 1919)
'Rolandslied' (French version)
'Karlamagnus saga' (1250)

al-Abd: One of the nine swords of the prophet Muhammad in Islamic legend. The name of this sword means 'cutting' or 'sharp'. According to legend, the sword was sent to Muhammad by one of his companions just before the Battle of Badr, and was used during the Battle of Uhurd.

A relic said to be the sword is currently in the Husain mosque in Cairo, Egypt.

al-Battar: One of the nine swords of the prophet Muhammad in Islamic legend. It was taken as booty from the Banu Qaynaqa, and is said to be the sword originally used by King David to decapitate the giant Goliath. Its name means 'the beater'.

al-Battar is also called the 'Sword of the Prophets', its blade is 101 cm in length, and it is engraved in arabic with the names of David, Solomon, Moses, Aaron, Joshua, Zecharia, John, Jesus, and Muhammad himself. The blade also sports an image of King David chopping the head off Goliath

Islamic legend has it that when Jesus returns to defeat the anti-Christ 'Dajjal', he will come and claim this sword.

A relic said to be the sword is preserved in the Topkapi Museum in Istanbul.

al-Ma'thur: Also known as the 'Ma'thur al-Fiqar', this is one of the nine swords of the prophet Muhammad in Islamic legend. It is said that this is the sword Muhammad used before he received revelations in Mecca, and that his father gave the sword to him.

The blade is 99 cm in length, and the handle is of gold in the shape of two serpents, encrusted with emeralds and turquoise.

A relic said to be the sword is preserved in the Topkapi Museum in Istanbul.

al-Rasub: One of the nine swords of the prophet Muhammad in Islamic legend. This particular sword has a blade that is 140 cm long and engraved with gold circles that have written on them the name Ja'far al-Sadiq.

A relic said to be the sword is currently preserved in the Topkapi museum in Istanbul.

al-Samsama: Sword of Amr b. Ma'dikarib al-Zubaidi (Amr bin Maadi Karib) nicknamed Abu Thaur, 'Father of the Bull.

al-Qadib: One of the nine swords of the prophet Muhammad in Islamic legend. The sword is a sword of defense or companionship for the traveller, and not meant to be used in battle.
Written on the side of the sword in silver is the inscription "There is no god but God, Muhammad the apostle of God—Muahammad b. Abdalla b. Abda al-Muttalib'.

The sword was said to have remained within the house of the prophet and was only used later by the Fatmid caliphs.

A relic said to be the sword is preserved in the Topkapi museum, Instanbul, and this sword has a blade that is 100 cm in length and has a scabbard of dyed animal hide.

Amanonuboko: The spear used by the gods Izanagi and Izanami to create the islands of the Japan, from the Japanese Shinto religion. The name means 'Marsh Halberd of Heaven' or 'Heavenly Jeweled Halberd'.

Legend has it that the gods stood at the bridge of heaven and used the spear to churn the waters of the sea. When they withdrew the spear, the first drops of salt water fell down to the world and became Japan.

Ame no Murakumo no Tsurugi: *See Kusanagi-no-tsurugi.*

Amenoohabari: Also known as the "ten-span sword", or "Itsu no ohabari no kami" in the *Kojiki*, and the "Ame no iwaya ni sumu kami", and the "Itsu no ohashiri no kami" in the *Nihongi*.

The Amenoohabari is a sword from Japanese myth and lore that was used by the god Izanagi to behead his newborn son the fire god Kagutsuchi because his wife Izanami suffered such terrible burns during the delivery that Izanagi was enraged. When the blood dripped from the point of the Amenoohabari, it transformed three rocks into several other deities associated with fire, thunder and swordmaking—Takemikazuchi, Iwasaku and Nesaku.

Amulet: An object that has been blessed by supernatural forces to protect the owner of the item.

In most of Europe it was believed that a pregnant woman was suspetible to attack from evil spirits, demons and witches. Expectant mothers often wear a plethora of amulets and charms to protect themselves from these supernatural attacks. At the time of conception, midwives would prepare a mother's bed with additional lucky charms, and sometimes even arrange for church bells to be rang at the time of birth.

Bibles were often carried as a protective amulet, and even today many soldiers will carry a pocket version with them for this purpose.

Sources:
'*Encyclopaedia of Superstitions, Folklore and the Occult Sciences, Vol. II*', by Cora Linn Daniels and C.M. Stevans, J.H. Yewdale and Sons Co. (1903)

<u>Andvarinaut</u>: A magical ring from Norse mythology capable of producing gold, but was also cursed. It was eventually owned by Sigurd, ultimately leading to his death.

The ring was first owned by Andvari. The mischievous Loki tricked Andvari into giving Andvarinaut to him. In revenge, Andvari cursed the ring to bring destruction to whoever possessed it.

Wanting to rid himself of the curse Loki quickly gave Andvarinaut to Hreidmar, King of the Norse dwarves, as a reparation: Loki and the other Æsir had inadvertently killed Hreidmar's son, Ótr. Otr's brother, Fafnir, then killed Hreidmar and took the ring. Sigurd later killed Fafnir and gave Andvarinaut to Brynhildr, who later killed herself when Sigurd left her.

The story of Andvarinaut is one of the central themes of Richard Wagner's *Der Ring des Nibelungen* (*The Ring of the Nibelung*).

Sources:
Encyclopedia of Mythology, Arthur Cotterell

Angervadil: (Also spelled Angurvddel). Angervadil is a sword that appears in the 14th century Norse epic *'Friðþjófs saga hins frœkna'*, which was sumarized in the 19th century poem *'Fridthjof'd Saga'*. Both stories tell of events that supposedly took place in the 8th century, and detail the story of Frithjof the Bold (Frithiof), who owned the sword.

The name 'Angervadil' means 'stream of anguish' or 'grief-wader'. Its nickname was 'brother of lightning'. Etched into the blue steel blade were runic letters that blazed red in battle but gleam a dim light during times of peace.

Angervadil was one of the three most treasured possessions of Frithjof, and it was passed down to him from his father. It was said to have been forged in the 'far away East' and tempered in fire by the dwarfs.

Frithjof used the sword to win many battles, and eventually became King of Rigerike.

Sources:
'Fridthjof'd Saga by Esais Tegne'r' (Swedish poem)

Apples of Youth: In Norse mythology, the apples which kept the gods strong and youthful. They were guarded by Idun, the wife of Bragi, god of poetry. The fire god Loki was once coerced by the frost giant Thiassi to steal the apples. Thiassi took them to Jotunheim, the land of the frost giants. This resulted in the gods becoming old and weak, which resulted in Odin forcing Loki to regain the apples and bring them back to the gods.

Source:
Encyclopedia of Mythology, Arthur Cotterell

Apollo's Bow: The silver bow of the Greek and later Roman god Apollo.

Apollo, like his sister Artemis (Diana to the Romans), was skilled in archery, and it is with his bow that he inflicted disease upon men. In Homer's *'Illiad'*, he is described as poisoning his arrows with plague and firing them at the Greeks to punish King Agamemnon for abducting the daughter of Apollo's high priest, Chryses.

The bow was one of the most important symbols of Apollo, and he had been known to bestow wonderous bows to mortals at times. The bow of Odysseus had originally been gifted by Apollo to King Eurytus of Oechalia (*See 'Odyssesus, Bow of'*). The Greek hero Heracles also received a bow from Apollo.

Source:
'Illiad', Homer

Argo: The ship featured in the classic Greek tale Jason and the Argonauts. Argo was the ship on which Jason and the Argonauts sailed from Iolcos to retrieve the Golden Fleece. She was named after her builder, Argus.

Argo was constructed by the shipwright Argus, and its crew were specially protected by the goddess Hera. The best source for the myth is the Argonautica by Apollonius Rhodius. According to a variety of sources of the legend, Argo was said to have been planned or constructed with the help of Athena. According to other legends she contained in her prow a magical piece of timber from the sacred forest of Dodona, which could speak and render prophecies. After the successful journey, Argo was consecrated to Poseidon in the Isthmus of Corinth. She was then translated into the sky and turned into the constellation of Argo Navis.

<u>Ark of the Covenant:</u> A container said to house the stone tablets containing the Ten Commandments, as featured in Abrahamic religions.

Also known as the Ark of the Testimony, it was described as a wooden chest clad with gold containing the two stone tablets as well as, according to various texts within the Hebrew Bible, Aaron's rod and a pot of manna which the Isrealites ate to sustain themselves during the Exodus.

The Scriptural account relates that, roughly twelve months following the Israelites' exodus from Egypt, the Ark was produced based on the pattern provided to Moses by God once the Israelites were encamped at the feet of the biblical Mount Sinai.

According to the New Testament Letter to the Hebrews, the Ark also contained Aaron's rod, and a jar of manna; however, the first of the Books of Kings says that at the time of King Solomon, the Ark contained only the two stone tablets.

Ascalon: The sword of Saint George used to slay a dragon in the European medieval folktale 'George and the Dragon'. The sword is supposedly named after the ancient city sea-port of Ashkelon, Israel.

The story goes that a dragon made a nest near a spring that provided the city-state of Silene, Libya with water. This made it impossible for anyone in the city to gather water without being attacked by the dragon, so they needed to lure the dragon away from the nest temporarily every day; this was accomplished by offering a "human offering" for the dragon to feast on—a virgin girl.

The victim of the day was chosen by drawing lots, and after several days a local princess ended up drawing the short end of the stick. The local Monarch begs to the townspeople for the princess life, but having already given up many of their own daughters they could not be persuaded. The princess is offered to the dragon but the sacrifice is interrupted by a knight-errant named George who proceeds to engage the dragon while mounted on a horse. Using his magical sword 'Ascalon', George saves the day. The townsfolk, inspired by the hero, then leave behind their "pagan ways" and convert to Christianity—the religion of George the Dragon-slayer.

For a long period of time, this story used to be considered a true account of a real person and a real event, but this belief has been abandoned in modern times. The story is now believed to have been a fictional story infused with religious symbolism, with George representing Christianity and the dragon representing witchcraft and paganism that Christianity was/is constantly trying to stamp out.

The story may be derived from other pre-Christian mythological tales, such as the Greek myth of Andromeda and her future husband Perseus who slays the Medusa, or the Babylonian myths of the god Marduk slaying the dragon Tiamat. Also of interest, in Sweden the tale of Saint George is supposed to represent an actual event: the princess represents Sweden, and the dragon represents an invading army. This accounts for why Sweden is full of several famous statues of Saint George battling the dragon.

In 1348 A.D., King Edward the III of England, a staunch promoter of chivalry, founded the 'Order of the Garter' and made Saint George the 'patron saint of England'. Saint George began to be seen as the original 'knight in shining armor'— an idealization of the spirit of chivalry which supposedly had existed in the Britain of past. The chapel at Windsor Castle is dedicated to Saint George.

"Saint George and the Dragon" by Thomas Maybank from The Book of Knowledge, p. 961, Vol. III, The Grolier Society, New York, 1911

Sources:
Seven Champions of Christendom, Richard Johnson (1596-7)

Ash Spear of Peleus: A spear described in the Illiad.

"At the marriage of Peleus and Thetis, the gods gathered together on Pelion to feast and brought Peleus gifts. Kheiron gave him a stout ashen shaft which he had cut for a spear, and Athena, it is said, polished it, and Hephaistos fitted it with a head. The story is given by the author of the Cypria." - Homerica, The Cypria Frag 5 (from Scholiast on Homer's Iliad 17.140)

Source:

'Illiad', Homer

Assal, Spear of: A spear that once belonged to the Irish god Lugh. The sons of Tireann had to retrieve the spear as punishment for killing Cian. When the spear was thrown in battle and the word 'ibur' shouted, the spear of Assal would always hit its target. When the word 'athibar' was spoken, it would return to the person who threw it.

Astra: Legendary weapons in Hindu mythology that can be channeled into ordinary objects, often arrows.

Of all magical weapons, Astras are closer to being a direct manifestation of supernatural power rather than a tool that supernatural power operates through. In a literal sense any object an Astra is channeled into becomes the Astra.

Astras are capable of extrodinary feats and could trigger natural disasters, such as hurricanes, earthquakes and even the destruction of the universe itself.

Astra are the weapons of deities, and are invoked into the mortal world by use of a specific invocation. This invocation could be taught to mortals, and in many Hindu sagas, such as the Ramayana and Mahabharata, the heroes often learn these invocations either from priests or from a god.

The use of an astra required specific conditions to be met, and if these conditions were not heeded the summoner could be killed.

The following is a list of various astras:

Aindraastra: Astra of Indra, God of weather. Can bring down a divine shower of arrows from the sky.

Agneyastra: Astra of Agni, God of fire. The weapon would release divine flames that cannot be extinguished normally.

Varunaastra: Astra of Varuna, God of water. The weapon would release massive volumes of water, and was typically invoked to counter Agneyastra.

Nagaastra: Astra of the Nagas. The weapon would have an ineering aim and take on the form of a snake, proving deadly upon impact.

Nagapaasha: Astra of the Nagas. Upon impact, this weapon would bind the target in coils of living venomous snakes. It was used in the Ramayana, against Rama and Lakshmana by Indrajit.

Vayvayaastra: Astra of Vayu, god of wind. It brought about a gale capable of lifting armies off the ground.

Suryastra: Astra of Surya, God of the sun. It created a dazzling light that would dispel any darkness.

Vajra: Astra of Indra, God of weather. The target would be struck with bolts of lightning.

Mohini: Astra of Mohini, an avatar of Vishnu. It dispelled any form of maya or sorcery.

Twashtar: Astra of Twashtri, the heavenly builder. When used against an army, it would cause them to mistake each other for enemies and fight one another.

Sammohana / Pramohana: Would cause entire armies to collapse in a trance.

Parvataastra: Would cause a mountain (parvata) to fall on the target from the skies.

Brahmaastra: Astra of Brahman, the Creator. Would destroy an entire army instantly, and could counter most other astras.

Brahmasirsha: Astra of Brahman, the Creator. Capable of killing devas (gods). Was used by Ashwatthama on Parikshit.

Narayanaastra: Astra of Vishnu, the Preserver. Would create a shower of arrows and discs. The astra's power would increase with the resistance offered to it. The weapon had to be obtained by Vishnu directly, and could be used only once.

Vaishnavaastra: Astra of Vishnu, the Preserver. Would destroy the target completely, irrespective of the target's nature. It was undefendable. It had to be obtained directly from Vishnu.

    Pashupatastra: Astra of Shiva, the Destroyer. Same effect as Vaishnavaastra.

Source:
The Ramayana
The Mahabharata
Srimad Bhagavastam

Arondight: (Also called 'Arondite', 'Aroundight', 'Altachiara', 'Chiarenza', 'Secace' or 'Gastiga-Folli') Sword of Sir Lancelot of the Lake in the Arthurian Norman romance 'Lancelot du Lac'. Lancelot used this sword to slay a 'fire-drake' (dragon).

Lancelot was attributed with other swords. According to pre-cycle *Lancelot*, the sword that Lancelot used against the Saxons at Saxon Rock was named '*Secace*', and it was also called Seure (Sequence) in Vulgate *Lancelot*.

In the 'L'Aspramonte', there is an account of a Jew who gave Charlemagne a sword that had an inscription claiming the blade had belonged to Lancelot and was named 'Gastigga-Folli', and later Sir Bevis of Hampton (with the name Bouvo d'Antona, in Yittish universe) would call the sword 'Chiarenza'.

In some tales it is also the sword of Guy, oldest son of Sir Bevis of Hampton, which he wielded in a battle between Bevis followers and the king's loyalists in London.

"Sir Guy strode (the back) of an Arabian horse tightly,
The horse was big and not light,
Sir Bevis with his own sword,
Which he had won in the Holy Land
A noble sword he had gone and taken for himself,
That was Lancelot of the Lake's
In the hilt was a carbunkle stone,
A better sord there never was one,
That any man has known to this day,
Except Bevis' good sword Morglay."

Sources:
The Romance of Sir Beus of Hamtoun (London:Pub for Early English Text Society by K.Paul, Trench, Trubner & Co, 1885, 1886)

L'Aspramonte, Andrea da Barberino (1370)

Le Marriage de Roland (1859)

Brewer's Dictionary of Phrase and Fable

<u>Artemis' Bow</u>: The golden bow of Artemis, Greek Goddess of hunting, wild animals, children and birth. She was known as Diana to the Romans.

"Over the shadowy hills and windy peaks she draws her golden bow, rejoicing in the chase, and sends out grievous shafts." Homeric Hymn 27 to Artemis

<u>Artemis' Spear</u>: The hunting spear of the Greek goddess Artemis.

Although quite seldom, Artemis is sometimes portrayed with a hunting spear. Her cult in Aetolia, the Artemis Aetolian, often portrayed her with a hunting spear.

Source:
Nonnus, Dionysiaca 48.302

<u>Azoth</u>: The sword of the legendary alchemist, physician, metallurgist, and astologer Paracelsus (1494-1541), whose real name was Theophhrast von Hohenheim.

The sword was believed to be between 110 and 130 centimeters long, which was rather large for the time and very unwieldly for combat purposes. The black pommel of the blade bore the inscription 'AZOTh', which gives it its name.

'AZOTh' was a word that meant 'Philosopher's Mercury'. In alchemic lore this described the elixir 'alexipharmakon' that served as a powerful counter-poison.

Nothing is known about how old the sword was, but legends surrounding Azoth claim that it was used to kill 82 Swedish nobles by Commander of Executioners Jorgen Homuth at the bequest of the Danish King Christian II who had recently conquered Sweden.

What is known for sure is that after Paracelsus came into possession of the blade, he ordered a series of engraving and woodcut portraits to be composed of himself holding the huge executioner's sword.

Because of the nature of the sword having been used to slay a mass amount of royals and being owned by a well-known alchemist, Azoth was attributed with various powers, two most important were,

1. The sword was said to contain the secret for curing diseases—a magical elixir was hidden inside the engraved pommel.

2. It was possessed by the spirits of the nobles it had been used to slain, and Paracelsus was able to command these spirits to perform magical workings for him.

3. Azoth was said to be able to transmute metals (such as creating silver).

Legend has it that Paracelsus lost the sword when assassins came to kill him in 1541. During Paracelsus lifetime, however, he was not viewed upon kindly because the sword was seen by many people as a symbol of betrayal, hatred and power—not to mention that the alchemist was known to be arrogant and have a sharp tongue.

In some of the more fanciful tales, 'Azoth' was the name of a demon that Paracelsus had trapped inside a crystal embedded in the pommel.

Where the sword currently is now, is hard to say. Some modern German Rosicrucian reconstructionists claim they have the blade, but have yet to publically present the sword.

Paracelsus with the Azoth

Source:

Rafal T. Prinke – "The Jagged Sword and Polish Rosicrucians" An article originally published in *Journal of Rosicrucian Studies*, 1 (1983), 8-13.

B

Babr-e Bayan: From Persian mythology, Babr-e Bayan was the name of the armor worn by the legendary Iranian hero Rostam. It was invincible against fire, water and weapons.

Balisarda: A sword that appears in the 16th century poem 'Orlando Furioso'.

Balisarda was the sword of the character Rogero, it was forged in the garden of Orgagna by the sorceress Falerina. It was forged for and given to Rogero so that he could kill Orlando.

The sword was capable of cutting through enchanted substances, such as armor or helmets.

*"With Balisarda's slightest blow,
Nor helm, norshield, no curass could avail,
Nor strongly-tempered plate, nor twisted mail"*

Source:
Orlando Furioso by Ludovico Artiosto (1516)
Brewer's Dictionary of Phrase and Fable

Bag, Santa Claus': The magical bag of Santa Claus that holds uncountable amounts of presents in it.

Santa Claus has his roots in the Norse god Odin. According to these beliefs, during the native Germanic holiday of Yule, Odin would lead a hunting party through the sky, riding his eight-legged horse Sleipnir. Children would fill their boots with an offering of carrots, straw or sugar, then leave them near the chimney to feed Sleipnir during the journey. Odin would then reward the children by replacing the offering with gifts such as candy. Thos practiced continued even after the European adoption of Christianity, instead becoming associated with Saint Nicholas as a result of Christianization of pagean beliefs—today this practice survives as the hanging of stockings on Christmas Eve.

The bag was originally held by servants of Odin to capture naughty children. When Odin was Christianized into Saint Nicholas, the servants become intertwined with legends of the shackled demon (the Krampus) Nicholas had subdued and made into his pet; other times, the servant was a slave of African origin who was owned by Nicholas. These traditions have survived modern times in the Netherlands, Flanders, Switzerland and Austria. These servants have been Americanized today as the Christmas elves.

<u>Balmung</u>: *See "Gram"*.

<u>Balin, Sword of</u>: Not the actual name of the sword, but a cursed sword that appears in the 'Le Morte d'Arthur" Arthurian stories written by Sir Thomas Mallory, a fifteenth century poet.

Balin, or 'Balia of the Two Swords', 'Knight of the Two Swords', or 'Balin the Savage'—all of which are titles Malory attributes to the character.

Balin was a Knight who underwent a trial of virtue which required him to remove a cursed sword that a lady had long worn, and only Balin was capable of removing it. Lady Lile of Avalon told him that if he chose to hold onto it, rather than return it, someday he would kill the one he loved most, but Balin did not believe in the curse.

However, the knight ended up accidentally killing his brother 'Balan' while both of them were covered in magical suits of armor that hid their identities from one another until it was too late—and both brothers delivered a fatal blow to one another at the same time. After their deaths, Merlin, the court wizard of King Arthur, buried the two brothers together.

Source:
'Le Morte d'Arthur" by Sir Thomas Mallory

Balswenden: (Palswende) The sword of Targis of Tortose, one of the Saracen counts of Marsilies, which he swears to kill the hero Ruolant (Roland) with.

Sources:
Grandes chroniques de france (1455-1460)
Rolandslied
Karl der Grosse

Baptism: One of the swords of Fortinbras (also known as 'Fierabras', or 'Strong-i-the-Arm' in some tales; the later is an English translation of what

Fierabras means in French) from the Matter of France tales.

In the French 'Fieranras' poem that talks about Fortinbas (here called Fierabras) Baptism was taken from him by Oliver when the latter temporarily lost his sword Hauticlere in battle. Oliver uses Baptism to defeat Fortinbas.

Baptism was described as possessing a golden hilt.

Sources:
Charles the Grete (15th century English translation of Fieranras)

La Chanson de Roland (circa 1100) translation by Charles K.Scott-Moncrieff

<u>Beans, Magic:</u> The magic beans from the fairy tale *Jack and the Beanstalk*.

Beans are historically associated with death. The romans ate beans during funerals and made offerings of beans to the dead. The flowers of beans are said to contain the souls of the dead. It was considered unlucky to smell the blossom of broad beans.

Sources:
Encyclopedia of Superstitions

<u>Begallta</u>: The sword of Diarmuid (The Bright Face) O'Duibhne. Begallta means 'Little Fury'. Diarmuid shattered the sword against the back of a mighty boar. After a hard battle, Diarmaid eventually drove

the broken blade into the boar's eye, killing it, but he himself was mortally wounded and died shortly thereafter.

Source:
"In the Celtic Past" by Ethna Carbery, Dublin, 1904

Beierlant: Sword of Treferis, a vassal of King Merzian, who sought to kill Wolfdietrich.

"Treferis the heathen came driving forth,
He wagged in his hand a sword named Beirerlant,
With which many Christians, in all his days,
And noble knights too, he smote to death."

Sources:
Detushes Heldenbuch

Der Grofe Wolfdietrich, A. Holtzmann (Heidelberg, 1965)

A Catalogue of Person's names in German Heoric Literature. Gillespie, George T

Berting: (Bertinng, Bierting, Birting) A sword that Orm receives from his deceased father to contest the marriage of the Giant of Berm (Perm in Russia), Bermeriss to the daughter of the Danish king.

After Orm defeats the giant, he ails to Iceland and faces Aland and Gerd, but is locked in stalemate until a mermaid tells him,

"Thy sword in spell is bound,
But swing it three times around thy head,

And stick it in the ground."

Orm does so and with one swing, the heads of both giants fall to the ground.

In one version of the tale, Orm kills Tord of Valland (the murderer of Orm's father) with the sword to appease his deceased spirit.

Sources:
'The Giant of Bern and Orm Ungerswayne', a ballad by George Burrow

Blarney Stone: A block of bluestone built into the battlements of Blarney Castle, Blarney about 8 km from Cork, Ireland. According to legend, kissing the stone endows the kisser with the gift of gab (great eloquence or skill at flattery). The stone was set into a tower of the castle in 1446. The castle is a popular tourist site in Ireland, attracting visitors from all over the world to kiss the Stone and tour the castle and its charming gardens.

The word blarney has come to mean clever, flattering, or coaxing talk.

Blue Dragon: *See "Green Dragon Crescent Blade".*

Blutgang: (Blodgang) Sword of Hieme (Heimr) from the Thidrekssaga Saga.

Heime's real name was Studas the Younger, and gave himself the name of Heime because it was the most fearsome dragon in the world. Heime left his father, Studas the Elder, but not before he had given Heime the sword Blutgang.

However, Blutgang was not all that special, and its blade broke into two pieces in the first battle Heime had against Thiorek, Heime surrendered to Thiorek and he was made a vassal.

Source:
Thidrekssaga

Bradamante, Spear of: A magical spear used by the female knight Bradamante, the greatest female knight in all of medieval literature. She was the sister of Rinaldo, in the Orlando Furioso tales. The spear had the power to unhorse everyone it touched.

Brahmastra: The arrow of Brahma, one of the most powerful weapons in Hinduism. The Brahmashirsha astra and Brahmanda astra were similar weapons, created to be even more powerful.

As referred to in many tales, it had been regarded as a very destructive weapon. It's stated that whenever the Brahmastra was released, there is neither a counterattack nor a defense that may stop it, except by another Brahmastra, Brahmashirsha astra, or perhaps a Brahmanda astra.

The Brahmastra never skipped its mark and needed to be utilized with very specific intent against an enemy or military force, because the target would face complete annihilation. It had been thought to become acquired by meditation upon the The almighty Brahma, or from the Guru who understood the invocations. Based on ancient Sanskrit documents, the Brahmastra is invoked with a search phrase or invocation that's presented upon the consumer when with all this weapon. The consumer would need to display immense mental concentration. It was only able to be used once per day.

Breastplate of the High Priest: Also know as the "Breastplate of Judgment", this was golden breastplate adorned with twelve jewels that was worn by the High Priest of the Isrealites, as recorded in the Old Testament (Exodus 28:17-20).

It is difficult to say what the twelve jewels were as some Hebrew words have multiple meanings. The most common interpretation is sard, topaz, carbuncle, emerald, sapphire, jasper, jacinth, agate, amethyst, chrysolite, onyx and beryl.

Passages in Exodus (28:21) indicate that the twelve stones are represenative of the twelve tribes of Israel, and a name of a tribe was engraved into a stone, but does not elaborate on which stones correspond to which tribe.

The Breastplate of the High Priest itself is little heard of today, but the idea of it can be felt in the form of "birthstones". Over the centuries, various writers would elaborate on the symbolism of the stones, associating them with the twelve months of the year as 'birthstones'. The first to do this was Josephus, a first century Jewish historian. He wrote that each stone contained a specific virtue that could be related to people born in different months, and named these stones as "Sardonyx, Topazos, Smaragdos, Anthrax, Jaspis, Sappheiros, Liguros, Amethystos, Achates, Chrysolithos, Onyx, Beryllus."

In the King James version of the Bible, the list was adjusted to "Sardius, Topax, Carbuncle, Emerald, Sapphire, Diamond, Ligure, Agate, Amethyst, Beryl, Onyx, Jasper."

The 1963 New World Translation reads the list as "Ruby, Topax, Carbunckle, Emerald, Sapphire, Jasper / Diamond, Hyacinth / Leshem, Agate, Amethyst, Beryl, Onyx and Jade."

Later, the National Association of Jewelers created their own list in 1912, but all jewelers did not accept this list. Consequently there are today many different lists of "birthstones", many of which are based on the readily available stones to the jeweler, and little to do with the actual Breastplate of the High Priest myth.

According to the Gemological Institute of America, the actual custom of wearing a stone because of its association with a month began in 1562 in Germany, although it may have also started in eighteenth century Poland. However, in the 16th and 17th century it was also popular for people to wear the stone of a month in order to gain therapeutic benefits of that specific stone. Gradually, it became more traditional to wear only the stone that corresponded to the month you were born in.

Due to these differing ideas about the jewels in the breastplate, there are many different ideas about what stone corresponds to each month, which explains why different "birthstone ring" manufacturers often sell different stones for a month than their competitors in order to capitalize on the ideas.

Sources
Encyclopedia of the Occult
Encylopedia of Superstitions

Bridle of Athena: A magical bridle given by the Greek goddess Athena to the hero Bellerophon, so he could tame the winged horse Pegasus.

Source:
Encyclopedia of Mythology, Arthur Cotterell

Brinnig: Sword of Hildebrand. The sword was used to wound Gernoz (Gernot) and to kill Gieselher.

In the Thidrekssaga, the sword is called "Lagulf" for some reason.

Source:
Thidrekssaga

Brionac: See Luin.

Brisingamen: The enchanted necklace of Norse goddess Freyja. It was said to be made of amber and when she wore it no one could withstand her charms.

Brisingamen was crafted by four dwarves (Alfrik, Berling, Dvalin and Grer), and as payment Freyja had to spend a night with each of them in turn.

C

<u>Caduceus:</u> The winged rod of the Greek Hermes, known to the Romans as Mercury.

It is described as a staff with two serpents entwined around the shaft and topped by wings. In modern times the Caduceus is associated with healing and is the emblem of medical doctors.

Heremes used the rod when escorting souls to the underworld. Legend says that the Caduceus is a symbol of reconciliation of arguments, for it was created when Hermes thrust it between two fighting snakes, who then wrapped around it and became joined together.

The symbol is older than the Greek mythos surrounding Heremes; the icon first appears in Mesopatamian cultures around 2,600 BC where the serpents represented a god of healing. This symbol moved from the Middle East and entered Greek culture. Imagery bearing similarties to the Caduceus also appear in ancient Indian temples as a symbol of the four elements: the wand being earth, the serpents representing fire and water, and the wings representing air.

In Hinduism, the caduceus is represantive of the transformation of spiritual conscieness through the body. The wand represents the spine, and the serpents the kundalini ("serpent energy") mystical force that resides in the earth.

Source:
Harper's Encyclopedia of Mystical and Paranormal Experience by Rosemary Ellen Guiley.

<u>Caladbolg</u>: Sword of the mythological Irish king Fergus mac Roich (sometimes spelled as Ferghus Mac Roich). Its name means "hard belly" or "hard lightning", but is sometimes also written as Caladcholg ("hard blade"). The sword was said to be as long as a rainbow and was capable of slicing the tops off hills by emitting a thunderbolt. In battle, one swing was enough to consume all that lay in its path.

It is a popular belief among folktale historians that Caladbolg was the fore-runner of King Arthur's sword Excalibur (See Excalibur).

Sources:
Tain Bo Cualgne (Cattle-Raid of Cooley)

<u>Cernwennan</u>: King Arthur's dagger as described in Welsh Arthurian legends.

Sometimes also called Carnwenhau ("white hilt"). It is attributed with the magical power to shroud its user in shadow.

In Culhwch and Olwen it us used to slay the witch Orddu by slicing her in half.

Source:

Matter of Britain
Culhwch and Olwen

<u>Chair, Saint Michael's</u>: A projecting stone lantern located in a town on St. Michaels' Mount, Cornwall. The tower has been erected there to commemorate the apparition of Saint Michael that appeared on that mount. It is believed that any woman who sits on the chair will rule her home as long as she lives. However, if after the ceremony her husband gets to the house before she returns, he will become the master of the home.

Sources:
'Encyclopaedia of Superstitions, Folklore and the Occult Sciences, Vol. II', by Cora Linn Daniels and C.M. Stevans, J.H. Yewdale and Sons Co. (1903)

<u>Chandrahas</u>: The sword of Ravana in the Indian epic "Ramayana". Ravana was given the sword by the King of the Gods, Shiva, as a reward for Ravana's bravery and devotion to him. The sword was said to be extremely powerful, and Ravana. Chandrahas means "Moon Blade",

Source:
Goldman, Robert P., *The Ramayana of Valmiki: An Epic of Ancient India* Princeton University Press, 1999 ISBN 0-691-01485-X

Arya, Ravi Prakash (ed.). *Ramayana of Valmiki: Sanskrit Text and English Translation.* (English translation according to M. N. Dutt, introduction by Dr. Ramashraya Sharma, 4-volume set) Parimal Publications: Delhi, 1998 ISBN 81-7110-156-9

Chrysaor: A magic sword made of adamant that appears in "The Faerie Queene" (1596), written by Edmund Spenser, a sixteenth centuy English Elizabethan poet. The sword was given to Sir Artegal, the Knight of Justice, by the Goddess Astraea, who had kept it since ancient times.

The sword had once belonged to Zeus (Jupiter) who had used it to defeat the Titans. Its blade was golden and tempered with Adamant, and capable of cutting through anything. The name means 'as good as gold'.

*"Which steely brand, to make him dreaded more,
She gaue vnto him, gotten by her slight,
And earnest search, where it was kept in store,
In loues Jupiter's eternall house, wvnwist, vnwist of wight,
Since he himselfe it vs'd in that great fight
Against the Titans, that whylome rebelled,
Gainst highest heauen;
Chrysaor it was hight;
Chrysaor that all other swords excelled,
Well prou'd in that same day, when Iou those Gyants quelled.
For of most perfect metall it was made,
Tempred with Adamant amongst the same
And garnisht all with gold vpon the blade
In goodly wise, whereof it tooke his name
And was of no lesse vertue, then of fame.
For there no substance was so firme and hard,
But it would pierce or cleaue, where so it came;
Ne any armour could his dint out ward,
But wheresoeur it did light, it throughly shard."*

Some modern Arthurian folklorists confuse Chrysaor as an earlier name for 'Excalibur', but this is incorrect, and the sword first appeared in Edmund Spenser's tale.

Sources:
Fairie Queene, Book V (1596) by Edmund Spencer
The Complete Works in Verse and Prose of Edmund Spenser [Grosart, London, 1882]

<u>Cid, Shield of:</u> Shield of the Spanish hero Rodrigo Díaz de Vivar, also known as El Cid. The shield was said to have a "fierce, shining golden dragon" adorning it.

The shield was attributed to him in the poem *'Carmen Campidoctoris'*, a manuscript that was written anonymously, but is the earliest known poem about the hero.

Source
'Carmen Campidoctoris' ("Song of the Campeador")

<u>Clarent</u>: (Clarente) A magic sword belonging to King Arthur that appears in the "Alliterative Morte Arthure", a 14th century poem retelling the Arthurian legends. It later began to appear elsewhere.

In some tales, Clarent is said to be the sword Arthur pulled from a stone in London to become 'High King of Britain'. Whereas Excalibur was the sword for use in war, Clarent was the sword of peace, used for knighting.

The legend goes that Uther Pendragon, High King of England died without a heir and that there were many lords and nobles who claimed the throne. To end the dispute, depending on the telling either God or Merlin put a sword into a large stone, and whoever could withdraw the sword would be crowned High King of England. All of the men present tried to pull it out but were unable until a young boy named Arthur withdrew the sword effortlessly—thus becoming High King of England himself.

Some stories suggest Arthur was drawn to the sword or pulled it out at the bequest of Merlin, while the fifteenth century poet Sir Thomas Mallory claimed in his 'Le Morte d'Arthur' that the boy drew Clarent when he was looking for a sword for his foster brother Kay and came upon the 'sword in the stone', and it was at this time that Merlin told Arthur about his true lineage—that his father had been the true High King of Britain. Having withdrawn the sword from the stone gives Arthur the right to be the King.

In the poem 'Alliterative Morte Arthure', Mordred stole Clarent while Arthur was away at war, and it is with Clarent that Mordred kills King Arthur. Other legends suggest Clarent was the sword that Arthur had broken in battle, and that Excalibur was the replacement given to him by The Lady of the Lake (*See Excalibur*)

Some scholars suggest that the basis for the 'Sword in the Stone' stems from early bronze age sword casting methods—melted bronze would be poured into hollowed molds of hardened clay or stone. When the bronze had cooled and the mold halves are separated, a 'sword in the stone' would need to be removed from one of the halves. Some believe the tale of Arthur drew on this historical sword-making process for poetic inspiration.

"The Sword in the Stone" monument at Disneyland theme parks is based on the legend of Clarent.

Sources:
Alliterative Morte Arthure
Le Morte d'Arthur by Sir Thomas Mallory

<u>Clarmie</u>: Sword of Engelier of Bordeau (or Gascony), according to the German version of the Song of Roland.

Sources:
Karlamagnus saga (1250)

Claiomh Solais: (Also spelled An Claidheamh Soluis and On Clive Sullish) Known as the "Sword of Light", it was the sword of Nuada Airgeadlamh, a legendary High King of Ireland. According to legend, the sword was given to him by the 'battle-witch' Scathach.

The sword was said to be indestructible and capable of cutting enemies in half. Along with the Spear of Lugh, Dagda's Cauldron and the Stone of Fal, Claiomh Solais was one of the "Four Treasures of Ireland", also called the 'Hallows (Gifts) of Ireland'. The sword was said to have come from the 'Otherworld', and it was a living thing.

Claiomh Solais was based on the 'Sword of Naudu', an earlier 'Treasure of Ireland' that was said to be impossible to avoid being struck and wounded by its contact. It was owned by Naudu Airgetlam, the "Silver Hand".

The 'Hallows of Ireland' are important token in the study of European occult history because the current symbols of the four magical elements are a Sword, Spear, Cup, and Pentacle; all of which are based on the mythology of the 'Four Treasures of Ireland'—additionally, royal regalia of most European monarch countries are composed of four primary objects which correspond to the Hallows.

In some Arthurian legends that involve the 'quest for the Holy Grail', the Lady of the Lake who granted Arthur the sword Excalibur is said to be the 'Guardian of the Hallows of Kingship' and that

Excalibur itself was the Claiomh Solais (*see Excalibur*).

Like all the Hallows, only someone of noble birth or who was either King or a representative of the King could wield it.

Source:
The History of Ireland by Geoffrey Keating, D.D. . D. Comyn , P. S. Dinneen (ed), First edition [The first three of four volumes in the series.] David Nutt, for the Irish Texts Society London (1902-1914)

<u>Closamont</u>: A sword forged for Charlemagne by Galas in the Matter of France tales.

Sources:
Song of Roland, translation by Charles Scott Moncrief (London, 1919)
Rolandslied (French version)
Karlamagnus saga (1250)

<u>Colada</u>: Sword of El Cid, Rodrigo Diaz de Vivar, a great Spanish hero from the 11th century. Colada means "The Tap".

Colada was originally the sword of Count Ramón Berenguer II (Raymond Berenger) of Barcelona, but Cid took the sword as a war trophy when he defeated the Count in 1082 C.E.

"And the Count Raymond Berenger he hath compelled to yield;
  And reaping honor for his beard a noble prize hath made:

A thousand marks of silver worth, the great Colada blade."

Cid gave Colada to the husband of one of his daughters as a wedding present, but when Cid learned her husband had treated her badly he took the sword back and passed it on to Martin Antolinez., one of his trusted knights,

"Martin Antolinez drew forth Colada, the brightness of which flashed over the whole field, for it was a marvelous sword; and in their strife he dealt him a back-handed blow which sheared off the crown of his helmet, and cut away hood and coif, and the hair of his head and the skin also: this stroke he dealt him with the precious Colada."

Colada can be seen in the Army Museum (Museo del Ejercito) in Madrid, Spain; however there is a legend that says this sword is a fake, and the real Colada vanished in 1503 C.E.

The other legendary sword of El Cid was Tizona (*See Tizona*)

The sword Colada from the Royal Armory in Madrid

Source:
National Epics by Kate Milner Rabb (1896)

<u>Colbrandy's brond:</u> (sometimes also called Curtayne): Sword of Miles, second-born son of Sir Bevis, from the Bevis of Hamptoun stories. Sometimes the sword was called "Aroundight", which was the sword of Lancelot of the Lake. (*See "Aroundight"*)

Sources:
The Romance of Sir Beus of Hamtoun (London: Pub for Early English Text Society by K.Paul, Trench, Trubner & Co, 1885, 1886)

<u>Conchobar mac Ness, Shield of:</u> An old folktale from the Isle of Man entitled ""The Story of the Isle of Falga", based on the Ulster Cycle states:- "Conchobar, who had not yet become King of Ulster, but was an ambitious young man seeking to gain a

kingdom, consulted the famous oracle at Clogher as to how he might best attain his end. The oracle advised him to proceed to the Isle of Man and get Culann to make these weapons for him.

Conchobar did so, and prevailed on Culann to begin his task; but, while awaiting its completion, he sauntered one morning along the shore, and in the course of his walk met with a mermaid fast asleep on the beach. He promptly bound the syren, but she, on waking and perceiving what had happened, besought him to liberate her; and to induce him to yield to her petition, she informed him that she was Teeval, the Princess of the Ocean; and promised that if he caused Culann to form her representation on the shield surrounded with this inscription, 'Teeval, Princess·of the Ocean,' it would possess such extraordinary powers that when ever he was about engaging his enemy in battle, and looked upon her figure on the shield, read the legend, and invoked her name, his enemies would diminish in strength, while he and his people would acquire a proportionate increase in theirs. Conchobar had the shield made according to the advice of Teeval, and, on his return to Ireland, such extraordinary success attended his arms, that he won the kingdom of Ulster.

Culann accepted Conchobar's offer, referred to above, and settled on the plain of Murthemne, which was fabled to have been formerly situated beneath the sea. It was here that he was visited by Conchobar, accompanied by his Court and Cuchulainn."

Cornocopiea: Also known as the Horn of Plenty, it is a symbol of abundance and nourishment, commonly a large horn-shaped container overflowing with produce, flowers or nuts. The horn originates from classical antiquity, it has continued as a symbol in Western art, and it is particularly associated with the Thanksgiving holiday in North America.

In Greek mythology the infant **Zeus** had to be hidden from his father **Kronus**. In a cave on **Mount Ida** on the island of **Crete**, **Zeus** was cared for and protected by the goat **Amalthea** ("Nourishing Goddess"), who fed him with her milk. Zeus was powerful even as a baby, and while playing with his nursemaid accidentally broke off one of her **horns**, which then had the divine power to provide unending nourishment.

Coreuseuse: (Coreiseuse) Sword of King Ban of Benwick, father of Lancelot, a famous Knight of the Round Table. Coreuseuse means "Wrathful".

Source:
Le Morte d'Arthur

Corrougue: Sword of Sir Otuel, a Saracen champion from the Matter of France tales.

Sources:
Song of Roland, translation by Charles Scott Moncrief (London, 1919)

Cremave: Also called the "Revealer of Truth", or "Swearing Stone", this is a black flagstone located at Saints' Island, near Ireland. It is said that if a man suspected of a sin or crime is brought here and swears falsely, the stone will place a mark on him and his descendants for seven generations; if the suspected is innocent of the charges, there will be no mark.

Sources:
'Encyclopaedia of Superstitions, Folklore and the Occult Sciences, Vol. II', by Cora Linn Daniels and C.M. Stevans, J.H. Yewdale and Sons Co. (1903)

Crocae Mors: Latin for 'Yellow Death', it was the name that Geoffrey of Monmouth gave for the sword of Julius Caesar.

The blade of Crocae Mors was supposedly made of gold and unbreakable. It was so named the 'Yellow Death' because none could evade death after being wounded by it. This is from medieval mythology—there is no record that Julius Caesar ever had a sword named Crocae Mors, let alone a gold plated one used in battle.

Geoffrey claimed that the sword was entombed with a Briton slain by Julius in combat, Nennius, brother of Cassibellaun, king of the Britons.

It is possible that the weapon was created through oral retellings of the Roman Empire, or that it only existed inside the mind of Geoffrey until he put it to paper.

Source:

J. C. Crick, *The historia regum Britannie of Geoffrey of Monmouth. 4, Dissemination and reception in the later Middle Ages* (Cambridge, 1991)

<u>Cronus' Sickle</u>: The weapon of Cronus, which he used to harvest crops and which was also the weapon he used to castrate and depose his father Uranus. It was said to be made of adamant.

Uranus drew the enmity of Cronus' mother, Gaia, when he hid the gigantic youngest children of Gaia, the hundred-armed Hecatonchires and one-eyed Cyclopes, in Tartarus, so that they would not see the light. Gaia created a great sickle and gathered together Cronus and his brothers to persuade them to kill Uranus. Only Cronus was willing to do the deed, so Gaia gave him the sickle and placed him in ambush. When Uranus met with Gaia, Cronus attacked Uranus with the sickle by cutting off his genitals, castrating him and casting the severed member into the sea. From the blood (or, by a few accounts, semen) that spilled out from Uranus and fell upon the earth, the Gigantes, Erinyes, and Meliae were produced. From the member that was cast into the sea, Aphrodite later emerged. For this, Uranus threatened vengeance and called his sons *titenes* ("straining ones") for overstepping their boundaries and daring to commit such an act, and this is the source of the name *Titan*.

Cronus is sometimes confused with Chronos, the personification of time in Greek mythology. This has led to the modern day imagery associated with the Grim Reaper (See *Death, Scythe of*).

Source:
Brown, Norman O. *Hesiod: Theogony* .Prentice Hall; 1 edition (January 1, 1953) 978-0023153105

Crucifix, Christ's: According to a medieval legend, the first man, Adam, was lying sick in bed and nearing death. He went to his son Seth and asked him to go into Paradise and retrieve some oil from the Tree of Mercy. Seth went to Paradise but the archangel Michael denied Seth passage, telling him that the oil could not be given to men until one thousand years had passed. Instead, the angel handed Seth a wand and planted it upon the grave of Adam after his death. Seth obeyed the instructions and in time the wand grey to be a tree, flourishing until the time of Solomon.

Noting its unique properties, Solomon had the tree cut down and used to make a summer house; but the workmen could not fit or fashion it. The wood was cast into a stream in the royal garden and used as a bridge. When the Queen of Sheba visited Solomon she recognized the virtue of the wood and would not tread upon it, but instead fell down and worshiped it. The queen warned Solomon to beware of the tree, for on it would be hanged one whose death would spell the end of the kingdom of the Jews. Taking heed, Solomon then had the wood buried underground. Years later a well was dug above this place that became known as the Pool of Bethesda, the water of which derived its healing power from the tree as much as the descent of an angel. When Christ's ministry then came to an end, the tree brought itself above ground to the surface of the pool and was then used by the Jews to make the crucifix on which Christ died.

Naturally the tale is medieval fabrication as it has no record in prior history, but it makes a good bedtime story.

Sources:
'Encyclopaedia of Superstitions, Folklore and the Occult Sciences, Vol. II', by Cora Linn Daniels and C.M. Stevans, J.H. Yewdale and Sons Co. (1903)

Cupid's bow and arrows: The tools of Cupid, a Roman god of love. Cupid was the son of Venus, the goddess of love and equilevant of the Greek goddess Aprodite.

Cupid was said to have a quiver full of "arrowed desires" that could make a person fall in love with another, although some of his arrows would turn people away from those who fell in love with them.

Sources:
Encyclopedia of Mythology by Arthur Cotterrell

Curtana: Curtana means 'The Cutter', and there are two legendary swords named 'Curtana': (corrupted Latin for 'shortened')

1. The "Sword of Mercy" used in the coronation ceremony of British royal monarchs. The tip of its blade has been cut off. It is one of the "Three Swords of Justice" of British coronation regalia. It was forged at the bequest of Edward the Confessor.

2. The sword of Ogier the Dane in the Matter of France European medieval tales, although it is also spelled 'Courtain' in some versions. In the tales, Curtana was forged by Munifican and bore the inscription, *"My name is Curtana, of the same steel and temper as Joyeuse and Durendal"*.

Sources:
Bullfinch's Mythology, Legends of Charlemagne, Chapter 24
Song of Roland, translation by Charles Scott Moncrief (London, 1919)

D

<u>Daevi Khadga</u>: The "Divine Sword", this is a legendary weapon from Hindu mythology. It appears in the Shantiparva section of the Mahabharata; one of the three major ancient Sanskrit epics of India and considered the longest literary epic poem in the world.

Unlike most other mythological swords, the Daevi Khadga is not a forged sword but a cosmic monster-entity that takes the form of a sword. It was created by Brahma, the Creator God, as a dreadful monster that spread from a sacrificial fire. At the bequest of Brahma, the monster assumed the form of a blazing, sharp-edged sword when he said:

"The 'being' I have conceived is Asi. It shall effect the destruction of the enemies of the gods and restore the Dharma."

Brahma then gave the weapon to Rudra (a form of Shiva, another god) with the instructions that he was to slay all the sinners of the world and restore the Dharma ("Cosmic Truth" or "Law of the Universe").

Rudra used it to annihilate the Danavas, and then gave the sword to the God Indra, who passed it on to Manu, the first Holy King, who was advised to wield it with care and only use it to punish the transgressors of Dharma. From that point on, various heroes from Hindu mythology wielded it.

Source:
The Mahabharata of Krishna-Dwaipayana, translation by Kisari Mohan Ganguli

Daedalus, Wings of: The wax wings of Daedalus, from Greek mythology.

Daedalus was a brilliant engineer that had designed the labyrinth for King Minos to contain the minotaur within. However, Daedalus was imprisoned within the labyrinth for revealing its secrets, so he created wings of wax and feathers for himself and his son Icarus to escape with. Daedalus warned Icarus to not fly too close to the sun, but the boy did not heed the warning and plummeted to his death when the rays of the sun melted his wings.

Source:
Encyclopedia of Mythology, Arthur Cotterell

Dainsleif: A sword from the Scandinavian legend of 'Hedinn and Hogni".

The sword was forged by the dwarf Dain and wielded by Hogni, King of Denmark, in a series of battles which led up to the Ragnarok ('End of the Gods'), a massive war between the gods which causes the end of the current world and the rebirthing of a new one.

The blade was said to give wounds that would never heal and that once drawn it could not be sheathed until it had killed a man, much like Tyfring.

When King Hogni's daughter Hildr runs away with her lover, King Hedinn, Hogni declares war on the other king because he has been insulted. In the resulting battle between the two armies, King Hogni wields Dainsleif to massacre King Hedin's army in a day, but Hildr uses her magic to revive all the dead soldiers every night. Thus, the 'eternal battle' goes on for years until the Ragnarok occurs and the world ends.

Sources:
Hjandnings
Prosse Edda, written by Snorri Sturluson in 1220.

<u>Damocles, Sword of:</u> The story of Damocles is more of a fable or anecdote than a legend, but is notable enough to deserve mention here.

According to Roman writer and statesman Marcus Tullius Cicero (January 3, 106 BC – December 7, 43 BC), in the 1st Century B.C. there was a king named Dionysius I in the city of Syracuse, Italy. King Dionysius had among his court a courtier named Damocles who often flattered the king. One day King Dionysius overheard Damocles envying his position and wondering what it would be like to be King.

Irritated at the boy, King Dionysius decided to teach his courtier a lesson. The King invited Damocles to change places with him for a day, and Damocles jumped at the chance. Damocles held a banquet and feasted on the King's throne, but when he happened to glance upward toward the ceiling he noticed a sharp sword was dangling above him by a single thread tied to the ceiling. Damocles was horrified and jumped up from the throne.

"Are you surprised?" said Dionysius. *"I came to power by violence and I have many enemies. Every day that I rule this city, my life is in as much danger as yours is at this moment."*

Now that Damocles better understood what it felt like to be a King, Damocles became much more content with his life as a courtier.

"The Sword of Damocles", a famous painting by Richard Westall (1812), now housed in the Ackland Art Museum

Source:

Marcus Tullius Cicero, Cicero's Tusculan Disputations Also, Treatises On The Nature Of The Gods, And On The Commonwealth, translation by C.D. Yonge, New York: published by Harper & Brothers, Franklin Square, 1877

<u>Death, The Scythe of:</u>, A weapon which represented the Christian cultural interpretation of death as a "harvester of souls". The view states that death takes life as we do crops. The scythe was never discussed in detail and is more popular as a common day icon associated with the Grim Reaper.

The portrayal of the scythe originates from a Hellenistic etymological misconception relating the god Cronus with time. Cronos was a harvest deity who is often shown with a sickle, which he also uses to castrate his father, Uranus.

Etymologists from the Hellenistic period erroneously correlated Cronus with time due to the similarity with the prefix chrono-. From this mistake, Cronus was often depicted as Father Time, carrying a scythe, which is a harvesting tool related to the sickle.

The characters of Father Time and the Grim Reaper frequently overlap, leading to the common potrayal of the Grim Reaper brandishing a scythe.

<u>Destiny, Spear of:</u> *See 'Longinus, Lance of'.*

<u>Dionysus, Sceptre of</u>: *See 'Thyrsus'.*

Dish, Saint Finnian's: A plate that is regarded as a holy relic. It is said that anyone who makes a false oath on the dish will become striken with disease and die within the year.

Sources:
'Encyclopaedia of Superstitions, Folklore and the Occult Sciences, Vol. II', by Cora Linn Daniels and C.M. Stevans, J.H. Yewdale and Sons Co. (1903)

Dobrynya Nikitich, Whip of: A magical whip given to Dobrynya Nikitich by his mother.

The bylina begins with Dobrynya's mother telling the hero not to go to the Saracen Mountains, not to trample baby dragons, not to rescue Russian captives, and not to bathe in the Puchai River. Dobrynya disobeys his mother and does all of these things.

When he is bathing in the Puchai River, the dragon appears. Dobrynya has nothing to defend himself, and thinks he is going to die. Dobrynya then discovers "a hat of the Greek land" and uses it to defeat the dragon.

The dragon pleas for Dobrynya not to kill him and the two make a nonaggression pact. Once the pact is made, the dragon flies away and captures the niece of Prince Volodymir, Zabava Potyatichna.

When Dobrynya arrives at Kiev, Prince Vladimir tells Dobrynya to rescue his niece. Dobrynya makes it to the Saracen Mountains with the help of a magic whip given to him by his mother, and begins to fight the dragon.

Dobrynya fought the dragon for three days. On the third day of the bloody battle, Dobrynya feels like giving up and riding away, but a voice from heaven tells him to stay and fight for three more hours. After the three hours Dobrynya kills the dragon.

When he killed the dragon, the blood did not soak into the ground, and Dobrynya and his horse were stuck in the blood for three days. A voice from heaven told the hero to stick his spear into the ground and say an incantation. The blood was then swallowed by the earth and Dobrynya rescued Zabava.

Since Dobrynya is a peasant, he cannot marry Zabava and gives her to Alyosha Popovich. Dobrynya encounters a polyanitsa, Nastasia, and marries her instead.

Sources:
Bailey, James; Tatyana Ivanova (1998). *An Anthology of Russian Folk Epics*. Armonk, New York: M.E. Sharpe, Inc. ISBN 0585265798.

<u>Dragvendil</u>: A sword owned by Egill Skalla-grimsoon. Dragvendil is a family or heirlmoon sword, passed down in his family from generation to generation. It was given to him by Porolfrs (Egill's uncle and brother) and his father Skalla-Grimr. The sword originally belonged to Ketill Trout, another great Viking hero.

Source:
The Epic Hero by Dean A. Miller

Draupnir: A golden armlet possessed by Odin in Norse mythology. Its name means *The Dropper* in English.

The armlet was a source of endless wealth, since each ninth morning it had spawned eight more gold rings just like itself. Draupnir was forged by the dwarven brothers Brokkr and Eitri (or Sindri). Brokkr and Eitri made this ring as one of a set of three gifts which included Mjollnir and Gullinbursti. They made these gifts in accordance with a wager Loki made saying that Brokk and Eitri could not make better gifts than the three made by the Sons of Ivaldi.

In the end Mjollnir, Thor's hammer, won the contest for Brokkr and Eitri. Loki, refusing to honour the initial wager of his head, was punished by having Brokk seal his lips shut with wire.

In the *Gylfaginning* the ring was placed by Odin on the funeral pyre of his son Baldr:

Odin laid upon the pyre the gold ring called Draupnir; this quality attended it: that every ninth night there fell from it eight gold rings of equal weight.

The ring was subsequently retrieved by Hermóðr. It was offered as a gift by Freyr's servant Skírnir in the wooing of Gerd, which is described in the poem Skírnismál.

Dup Shimati: In Sumerian mythology these are the Tablets of Destinies. Whoever possessed the tablets ruled the universe.

They were described as clay tablets inscribed with cuneiform writing, also impressed with cylinder seals, which, as a permanent legal document, conferred upon the god Enlil his supreme authority as ruler of the universe.

In the Sumerian poem *Ninurta and the Turtle* it is the god Enki, rather than Enlil, who holds the tablets. Both this poem and the Akkadian *Anzû* poem share concern of the theft of the tablet by the bird Imdugud (Sumerian) or Anzû (Akkadian).

In the Babylonian *Enuma Elish*, Tiamat bestows this tablet on Kingu and gives him command of her army. Marduk, the chosen champion of the gods, then fights and destroys Tiamat and her army. Marduk reclaims the Tablet of Destinies for himself, thereby strengthening his rule among the gods.

Durandel: (Sometimes spelled Durendal, Durandal, Dyrumdali or Durindana) Sword of Roland (Orlando in Italian myths), one of the Twelve Peers and nephew of Charlemagne, from medieval legends. The original meaning of the name 'Durandel' is obscure, but its Italinized form 'Durindana' is interpreted to mean 'inflexible'.

In some tales it was said to have once belonged to Hector of Troy. Four versions exist on how Roland received it; some say Roland won it from the giant Jutmundus, and some say he received it from an enchanter named Malagigi/Maugris. A third tale says Munifican, who also forged Sauvaigne and Courtain, forged it.

The last tale comes from the Karlamagnus Saga, which says that Charlemagne received the sword from a banker as payment for releasing his brother, and Charlemagne gave the sword to Roland after receiving a vision from a messenger of God:

"The night after this, as Karlamagnus lay in his bed, the angel Gabriel came to him and told him that his sword contained a precious, holy relic: 'There is in it a tooth of Peter the Apostle, and a hair of Maria Magdalene, and some blood of Bishop Blasius; you shall give the sword to Rollant, your kinsman, for it will then be in good hands."

The manner in which Roland receives the sword is not the only difference between the poems: the precise relics contained in the hilt also tend to change depending on what source you look at.

In the Chanson de Roland, the sword is said to contain a tooth of Saint Peter, a hair of Saint Denis, a drop of St. Basil's blood and a thread from the cloak of the Blessed Virgin Mary.

"Relics enough thy golden hilt conceals:
Saint Peter's Tooth, the Blood of Saint Basile,
Some of the Hairs of my Lord, Saint Denise,
Some of the Robe, was worn by Saint Mary."

In the Rolandslied (Middle High German translation of the poem by a Bavarian priest named Konrad, 1170), a slightly different set of relics is set inside Durandel's hilt:

*"The emperor insisted that great power be sealed in your hilt:
St Peter's blood, relics of St. Blasus, some hair of St. Denys, and a piece of cloth from St. Mary's garment."*

Legend has it that during the Battle of Roncevaux Pass, Roland tried to destroy the sword to prevent it from being captured by enemy Saracen forces when his army was overwhelmed, but the sword proved indestructible and created what is now the mountain pass Le Breche de Roland in Pyrenees from the damage. Nearing death and frustrated, Roland gave up trying to break the sword and threw it into a poisoned lake instead.

Folk legend says the sword was recovered, and is preserved in Rocamadour, France.

Sources:
Various 'Chanson de Roland' tales

Le Mariage de Roland by Victor Hugo(1859)

Karlamagnussaga (Norse work written in the 13th century)

Karlamagnus Saga: The Saga of Charlemagne and his Heroes, translation by Hieatt, Constance B, Toronto: Pontifical Inst. Of Medieval Studies, 1975)

Rolandslied (1170)
Priest Konrad's Song of Roland, translation by J.W. Thomas, Columbia, SC: Camden House, 1994

Fierabras (1485)
Charles the Grete, translation, published by Caxton

Orlando Furioso (1516)
By Lodovico Ariosto, translated by William Stewart Rose

Dyrnwyn: (White-Hilt) The sword of Welsh King Rhydderch Hael the Generous, it is one of the 'Thirteen Treasures of Britain' in the Arthurian legends recorded in the 'Mabinogion' and early Welsh 'Triads of the Island of Britain' (Trioedd Ynys Prydein).

Dyrnwin was said to be "possessing the ability to burst into flame". If drawn by a worthy man the sword would help in his cause but if the sword was used for immoral acts, the fires of the blade would consume him on the spot.

As one of the Thirteen Treasures, or 'Hallows of Britain', it could only be used by the King or his represenative in battle.

Like the other Treasures of Britain, it was probably based on the Hallows (Gifts) of Ireland.

In some tales, Dyrnwyn, as with the other treasures, is said to be guarded by the wizard Merlin at Bardsey Island.

Sources:
'The Mabinogion', translated by Gantz, Jeffrey
London and New York, Penguin Books, 1976
'Trioedd Ynys Prydein: The Welsh Triads',
translation by Rachel Bromwich: Cardiff: University
of Wales Press, 1978

E

<u>Eckisax</u>: (Ekkisax) A sword used by King Dietrich of Bern in the Thidrekssaga. Dietrich gains it by killing its previous owner, a warrior named Ecke (or Ekka). Later, Dietrich uses the sword to overcome Hagen. Alfrek the dwarf, who had also forged the Nagelring, forged the Eckisax.

Sources:
'The Saga of Thidrek of Bern', translation by Edward R Haymes, New York: Garland, (1988)

Nibelungenlied, translation by Daniel Bussier Shumway, Houghton-Mifflin Co., New York (1909)

<u>Edward the Confessor, Ring of:</u> A ring made of amethyst that, according to English legend, belonged to King Edward "the Confessor" of England. It had the power to guard the wearer from all contagious diseases.

The story goes that King Edward was on his way to Westminster when he encountered at the side of the road a beggar who implored him, in the name of Saint John the Baptist, to spare him some aid. In a most charitable spirit the king removed from his own finger an amethyst ring of great value and handed it to the man, who then vanished in a cloud of smoke.

Many years later, two pilgrims in the Holy Land found themselves lost in the desert when a long-bearded man suddenly appeared before them and announced he was Saint John the Baptist. The saint gave the men the ring of King Edward and told them to return it, and then inform the king that soon the saint would meet him in Heaven. The two men returned to England and presented King Edward with the ring. A few weeks later the king died.

For many years the ring was preserved as a sacred relic by the church of Haverling until the stone was set into the British royal crown.

Sources:
'Encyclopaedia of Superstitions, Folklore and the Occult Sciences, Vol. II', J.H. Yewdale and Sons Co. (1903)

<u>Eros, Arrows of</u>: The arrows of Eros, the Greek god of love. Eros had two types of arrows, gold tipped and lead tipped. The golden arrows would make anyone, even a god, immediently fall in love with another person, while the lead arrows would make someone incapable of feeling love.

As punishment for being harassed by Apollo, the god of prophecy, Eros shot him with a golden arrow that made him fall in love with a nymph named Daphne, while Daphne was shot with a lead tipped arrow so that she could never return Apollo's affections.

The Romans may have based Cupid on Eros, as Cupid also had arrows capable of the same effects. (See 'Cupid, Bow and Arrows of')

Source:
Encyclopedia of Mythology, Arthur Cotterell

<u>Excalibur</u>: Also spelled as Excaliber, the name roughly means "Cut Steel". Excalibur is the legendary sword of King Arthur from European medieval myth and legend. Excalibur is arguably the most famous legendary sword, if not the most legendary weapon in the world.

The origins of how Arthur gained Excalibur are sometimes obscere. One popular accounts says that Arthur gained Excalibur when he pulled the sword from the stone to become king; but other stories suggest Arthur gained it from The Lady of the Lake after becoming king and the "Sword in the Stone" was a separate sword, sometimes named Clarent (See "Clarent").

The early Welsh Arthurian legends call Excalibur "Caledfwlch", which is a name that sounds very similar to another mythological weapon that shares traits with Excaliber, Caladbolg (See Caladbolg).

In the Welsh *'Mabinogion'* stories about Arthur, Caledfwlch was described as "....with a design of two serpents on the golden hilt; when the sword was unsheathed what was seen from the mouths of the two serpents was like two hot flames of fire, so dreadful that it was not easy for anyone to look."

Later, Geoffrey of Monmouth's *History of the Kings of Britain* speaks of the sword, saying that it was forged on the holy island of Avalon. Geoffrey latinized the name "Caledfwlch" to

"Caliburn/Caliburnus". The name continued to be corrupted through oral and written traditions until it became 'Escalibor'. The name finally became 'Excalibur' when Robert Wace, a twelfth century French poet, began writing about King Arthur and his 'Round Table'.

Despite its origins, the sword is usually agreed to possess many powers, among which was extraordinary cutting strength and durability. It was said to be only breakable if the wielder attempted to use it for anything except honorable acts.

Excalibur was also said to bear two inscriptions on opposite sides of the blade; one side said "Take Me Up" and the other said "Cast Me Away". The later engraving would be a prelude to the final days of Arthur's reign, where a dieing Arthur has a trusted knight, Sir Bedivere, throw the sword into the water to return it to the Lady of the Lake. There is evidence that it was customary to consider a warrior's sword singular to him, imbued with his spirit. Sometimes a sword would be thrown into a body of water to discourage its retrieval by an enemy, or anyone else.

While Excalibur was said to "guarantee victory" in battle, in some versions of the story it was the scabbard of Excalibur that was most important, for it was blessed to make the owner invincible to mortal wounds; they either did not die from bleeding or their wounds did not bleed. In these versions of the Arthurian legend, it is because Arthur lost the scabbard that Mordred could kill him.

Also worth note, that while latter tales say that only Arthur could wield Excalibur, some early Welsh and French tales had stories where some of Arthur's knights also bore Excalibur; for example, Gawain wielded the legendary blade in the 'Lancelot Proper' stories.

Some legends go further and say that Wayland the Smith, the blacksmith to the Norse gods who forged many wondrous items, forged Excalibur.

Arthur Obtains the Sword Excalibur: Daniel Maclise, 1857

Sources:
Lord Tennyson, Alfred; edited by J.M. Gray (1983). **Idylls of the King**. Penguin Classics. ISBN 0140422536.

Brewer's Dictionary of Phrase and Fable by Ebenezer Cobham Brewer,

J.S.P. Tatlock. *The Legendary History of Britain: Geoffrey of Monmouth's Historia Regum Britanniae and its early vernacular versions.* University of California Press. Berkeley. 1950.

Excalibur, Tuscan: The "Tuscan Excalibur" (or "Italian Excalibur" to some) is the name of an 800-year-old sword said to have belonged to the Catholic Saint Galgano Guidotti (1148 C.E. - 3 December 1181 C.E.). The sword is enshrined in the Abbey of Saint Galgano at Montesiepi, Italy.

The story goes that in 1180 C.E., a knight named Galgano had a vision from the Arch-Angel Michael that he should give up worldly possessions. Galgano responded that to do that would be as difficult as splitting a rock with a sword. To demonstrate what he meant, Galgano attempted to thrust his own sword into the rock expecting the blade to snap, but was shocked when the sword "slid like butter" into the stone. Inspired by the miracle, Galgano renounced his title and became a recluse. After Galgano was canonized a Saint in 1885 C.E., a shrine was built over the site of his sword. The shrine still exists today, as does the relic said to be his sword.

The sword was considered a fake for many years, but in 2001 C.E. the University of Pavia performed a study on the metal composition of the blade. Their research implied the sword lacked modern alloys and was compatible with that of a 12th century sword.

Legend has it that anyone who tries to remove the sword will have their arms supernaturally ripped out. However, it is known that the sword was easily removable from the stone until 1924 C.E., when the crevice was filled with lead.

The Tuscan Excalibur at the Abbey of Saint Galgano.

Source:
Piccinni G., *I mille anni del Medioevo*, Milano, Mondadori, 1999, ISBN 8842493554.

Eye of Balor: The single eyeball of Balor, had the power to kill with a glance. It is the root of the 'Evil Eye' superstition.

F

<u>Fairy Flag of Dunvegan:</u> According to legend, a scrap of cloth torn from the dress of a fairy who had married a chieftain of the MacLeods but had to leave mortal life after twenty years of marriage.

The flag is a heirloom of the chiefs of Clan MacLeod. It is held in Dunvegan Castle along with other notable heirlooms, such as the Dunvegan Cup and Sir Rory Mor's Horn. The Fairy Flag is known for the numerous traditions of fairies, and magical properties associated with it.

The flag is made of silk, is yellow or brown in colour, and measures about 18 inches (46 cm) squared. It has been examined numerous times in the last two centuries, and its condition has somewhat deteriorated. It is ripped and tattered, and is considered to be extremely fragile. The flag is covered in small red "elf dots". In the early part of the 19th century, the flag was also marked with small crosses, but these have since disappeared.

The silk of the flag has been stated to have originated in the Far East, and was therefore extremely precious, which led some to believe that the flag may have been an important relic of some sort.

Clan tradition, preserved in the early 19th century, tells how the Fairy Flag was entrusted to a family of hereditary standard bearers. Only the eldest male of this family was ever allowed to unfurl the flag; the first such hereditary standard bearer was given the honour of being buried inside the tomb of the chiefs, on the sacred isle of Iona. Tradition states that the flag was unfurled at several clan battles in the 15th and 16th centuries; the flag's magical powers are said to have won at least one of them. Another 19th century tradition linked the flag to a prophecy which foretold the downfall of Clan MacLeod; but it also prophesied that, in the "far distant future", the clan would regain its power and raise its honour higher than ever before. In the mid-20th century, the Fairy Flag was said to have extinguished a fire at Dunvegan Castle, and to have given luck to servicemen flying bombing missions in the Second World War.

Sources:
'The MacLeods of Dunvegan', MacLeod, Roderick Charles (1927)

Flamberge: Flamberge (also called Floberge) was the name of a sword from medieval myth and legend that was wielded by Renaud de Montauban (Rinaldo di Montalbano in *Orlando Furioso*). The smith Galas forged Flamberge, and it was one of the nine swords shattered by Hauteclere, sword of Oliver, one of the Twelve Paladins (peers) of Charlemagne in the 'Matter of France' tales. (*See Hauteclere*) Flamberge means 'Flame Cutter'.

In *"The Four Sons of Duke Aymon"*, the sorcerer Maugis took from Anthenor the Sacracen the sword Flamberge. He gave it to his cousin Renauld.

The legend of the weapon gave birth to the 'flambard' or 'flammard' model of sword blade, which is sometimes mistakenly called a 'flamberge'. Flambard swords have a wavy blade that somewhat resembles a flame, but is designed to cause painful vibrations in the hand of the enemy when it was used to parry their sword.

A flambard can be a one-handed sword, but is typically reproduced as a large two-handed Zweihander based on a sample from the 16th century.

Sources:
Song of Roland, translation by Charles Scott Moncrief (London, 1919)
Bullfinch's Mythology

Orlando Furioso by Ludovico Ariosto

<u>Flaming swords</u>: Swords which have blades made of fire or glowing with some kind of supernatural, magical power. They appear in many legends and myths; sometimes they have names and sometimes they do not.

An example of such a legend is from Hebrew mythologies (and their derivates, such as Christianity). It is said that an angel armed with a flaming sword was placed by God at the Gates of Paradise after Adam and Eve, the first humans, were banished from God's grace. (See *"Lightning Flash"*.)

Other flaming swords appearing in mythology include the Norse Fire Giant Surt's Laevateinn (See *"Laevateinn"*), King Rhydderch Hael's "Dyrnwyn" (*See "Dyrnwyn"*) the flaming sword of the Hindu Avatar Kalki, and the swords of the Valkyries. The Arch Angel Michael is also often depicted as wielding a sword of fire.

"The Archangel Michael Trampling the Devil Underfoot" painting by Simon Ushakov (1626-1686) The Tretyakov Gallery, Moscow, Russia

Flying Carpet: Also known as "Prince Housain's carpet", the magic carpet from Tangu in Persia.

Magic carpets have appeared in literature from almost Biblical times through the present day. The popularity of *One Thousand and One Nights* brought magic carpets to the attention of Western audiences. The literary traditions of several other cultures also feature magical carpets. The magic carpet of Tangu, also called "Prince Housain's carpet" was a seemingly worthless carpet from Tangu in Persia that acted as a magic carpet. It was featured in tales from *One Thousand and One Nights*.

King Solomon's carpet was reportedly made of green silk with a golden weft, sixty miles long and sixty miles wide: "when Solomon sat upon the carpet he was caught up by the wind, and sailed through the air so quickly that he breakfasted at Damascus and supped in Media." The wind followed Solomon's commands, and ensured the carpet would go to the proper destination; when Solomon was proud, for his greatness and many accomplishments, the carpet gave a shake and 40,000 fell to their deaths. The carpet was shielded from the sun by a canopy of birds. In Shaikh Muhammad ibn Yahya al-Tadifi al-Hanbali's book of wonders, *Qala'id-al-Jawahir* ("Necklaces of Gems"), Shaikh Abdul-Qadir Gilani walks on the water of the River Tigris, then an enormous prayer rug (*sajjada*) appears in the sky above, "as if it were the flying carpet of Solomon [*bisat Sulaiman*]".

In Russian folk tales, Baba Yaga can supply Ivan the Fool with a flying carpet or some other magical gifts (e.g., a ball that rolls in front of the hero showing him the way or a towel that can turn into a bridge). Such gifts help the hero to find his way "beyond thrice-nine lands, in the thrice-ten kingdom". Russian painter Viktor Vasnetsov illustrated the tales featuring a flying carpet on two occasions.

<u>Fragatach</u>: (Fragarach, Froach Mor) From Irish mythology, the sword called "The Answerer" or "The Retaliator". The gods forged Fragatach so that it

would control the powers of the winds, could break any armor and would never miss its target. It was also able to speak.

It was the weapon of the sea god Manannan mac Lir, who passed it on to his foster son, the High King Lugh Lamfada, who then gave it to Cuchulainn (another great Iris hero), and it later ended up in the hands of legendary High King Conn of the Hundred Battles.

Sources:
'Dictionary of Celtic Mythology', James MacKillop, Oxford University Press (1998)
'Aspects of the Tain', J.P. Mallory December Publications, Belfast (1992)

(Book of Invasions translation) 'Lebor Gabala Erenn', translation by R. A. Stewart Macalister, D. Litt. (1938-1956)

'Early Irish History and Mythology', T. F. O'Rahilly, Dublin Institute for Advanced Studies, 1946)

Free-balls: Also known as "Free-bullets", or "Freikugeln". Charmed bullets that would infallibly hit their targets. According to German superstition from the 14th and 15th century, these bullets were gifts to those who had performed pacts with the devil or one of his conjurers, and many old magic books and grimories contained rituals for how to attain them, often involving shooting silver bullets at pictures of the intended victim. The retrieved round would then be charmed.

The 13th century German folk tale of "Freischutz" recalls a legend of a marksman who used such bullets. Freischutz makes a pact with the devil to obtain seven bullets-- six that will hit without fail any object that Freischutz wishes to shoot, but the seventh is at the absolute disposal of the devil himself. The French also have a version of this tale known as "Robin des Bois".

The tale was very popular during the early 1800s when it was included with Johann August Apel's "Das Gespensterbuch" (Book of Ghosts, also known as Tales of the Dead), and then again when Weber made it into an opera in 1821 as "Der Freischutz".

Sources:
'Encyclopaedia of Superstitions, Folklore and the Occult Sciences, Vol. II', by Cora Linn Daniels and C.M. Stevans, J.H. Yewdale and Sons Co. (1903)

<u>Freyr's Sword</u>: The unnamed magical sword of Freyr, a god from Norse mythology. It was said to 'fight on its own if wise be he who wields it'.

Despite being such a great weapon, Freyr is easily parted with it—the god falls in love with a beautiful giantress named Geror, but is too bashful to woo her himself. Freyr begs his foot-page, Skirnir to go and woo the maiden for him, and Skirnir says he will do so if 'Freyr should give him his own sword which is so good that it fights for itself'.

Freyr then hands over his own sword to Skirnir, who is then compelled to successfully persuade Geror—a task the foot-page suceeds in.

However, the loss of Freyr's sword is the primary factor to why the now defenseless god is the first to fall in battle at the Ragnarok when the fire giant King Sutr overtakes him using his own sword, Laevateinn (See 'Laevateinn').

Artwork by Jacques Reich (1852 - 1923) showing the Norse god Freyr.

Sources:

'The Prosse Edda by Snorrir Sturluson' translation by Brodeur, Arthur Gilchrist, New York: The American-Scandinavian Foundation (1916)

'Saxo Grammaticus: The History of the Danes: Books I-IX' Davidson, Hilda Elis and Peter Fisher, Bury St. Edmunds: St Edmundsbury Press (1999)

Futsu no mitama: A sword given to the Japanese Emperor Jinmu by a kami named Amenokagoyama. During the Emperor's campaign to subdue the Central Land of Reed Plains, the Emperor and his army were subdued by sleeping poison emitted by "rough deities" at Kumano.

The goddess Amaterasu asked the god Takemikazuchi to assist the Emperor but rather than going himself, Takemikazuchi decided to send his magical sword Futsu no mitama to his earthbound son Takakuraji who was among the Emperor's forces. When Takakuraji awoke from his sleep, he found the sword just as the dream had foretold, and bore it to the Emperor Jinmu. The emperor and his forces opened their eyes, and using the sword they were able to defeat the rough deities.

Futsu no mitama is believed to represent a divine sword that is itself a deity, and it is worshiped by the martial clan Mononobe, who were instrumental in the early pacification of Japan, and is enshrined as the central deity (*saijin*) of Isonokami Jingū and other shrines.

G

Gae Bulg: (Also spelled Gae Bulga, Gae Bolg, and Gae Bolga) the spear of Cuchulainn from the Ulster Cycle of Irish mythology. The name means 'notched spear', 'belly spear', bellows-dart or 'lightning spear.

The spear was fashioned from the bone of the sea monster Coinchenn which had been killed by another monster, Curruid.

The spear required a special ritual in order for it to be used in battle. It needed to be washed in a stream and then cast from the fork of the toes. When it pierced the body of an enemy, the spear head would open into several barbs that tore through him.

The only way the spear could be removed was by literally cutting the dead man's body open.

Cuchulainn was given the spear by Scathach, a great female warrior who was Cuchulainn's teacher. Cuchulainn used it in many battles to emerge victorious.

Galatyn: (*Galatine*) The Sword of Sir Gawain from the Arthurian legends.

Source:
Le Morte d'Arthur

Gandiva: Also spelled as 'Gandeeva'. The bow of Arjuna, given to him by the Hindu God of Fire, Agni. The bow was given to Arjuna, an exceptional archer who could fire with either hand, to prevent the king of the gods, Indra, from extinguishing a fire caused by his rain. Arjuna later used the bow to kill many of his enemies.

The bow is known to be created from the wood of a heaven tree called the Gandi. It had more than a hundred strings allowing it to fire hundreds of arrows in one time ranging in distance over several miles. The body of the bow said to be indestructible.

There was only one bow in the land that could match the Gandivas existence, called the Vijaya it was held and wielded by Arjuna's arch enemy and older brother Karna.

Source:
The Bhagavad-Gita (Song of God)
The Mahabharate

Gjallarhorn: In Norse mythology, a drinking horn that was used by Mímir to drink from the well Mímisbrunnr (see *Mímisbrunnr*). It was to be used later by the god Heimdallr to announce the start of Ragnarök.

Gleipnir: The magic chain that bound the Fenris wolf in Norse mythology. It was light and thin as silk but strong as creation itself and made from six wonderful ingredients.

Gleipnir is mentioned in chapter 34 of the *Prose Edda* book *Gylfaginning.* The Gods had attempted to bind Fenrir twice before with huge chains of metal, but Fenrir was able to break free both times. Therefore, they commissioned dwarves to forge a chain that was impossible to break.

To create a chain to achieve the impossible, the dwarves fashioned the chain out of six supposedly impossible things:

The sound of a cat's footfall;
The beard of a woman;
The roots of a mountain;
The sinews of a bear;
The breath of a fish;
The spittle of a bird.

Therefore, even though Gleipnir is as thin as a silken ribbon, it is stronger than any iron chain. It was forged by the dwarves in their underground realm of Niðavellir.

Golden Apples: Often seen in Greek myths as a sacred fruit of the gods.

Golden apples were of the hesperides, the female guardians of the fruit that Gaira presented to Hera at her marriage to Zeus. Atlas offered to get them for Heracles if Heracles would take over his job of holding up the world. This was one of Heracles labors.

Also appear in the tale of Atalanta. Aphrodite took pity on a man named Malanion and gave him three gold apples to distract Atalanta with, so he could win a race against her to make her his wife.

Source: *Encyclopedia of Mythology* by Arthur Cotterell

Golden Fleece: The fleece of a gold-haired winged ram, which was held in Colchis. The fleece is a symbol of authority and kingship. It figures in the tale of the hero Jason and his band of Argonauts, who set out on a quest for the fleece by order of King Pelias, in order to place Jason rightfully on the throne of Iolcus in Thessaly. Through the help of the sorceress Medea they acquire the Golden Fleece.

Golden Harp: The enchanted harp from the English fairy tale '*Jack and the Beanstalk*'. The harp was capable of playing music by itself.

Gou Jian, Sword of: The Sword of Gou Jian, a famous king of the Yue Kingdom (510 BC-334 BC), is a real weapon over 2,000 years old from the Spring and Autumn Period of modern China.

The sword was unearthed in Hubei, China in 1965, during an archaelogical survey along the Zhang River Reservoir. It was discovered inside a burial casket along with a human skeleton.

The sword was sheathed in a wooden scabbard and had an almost air-tight it with the sword body. When the sword was unsheathed by researchers, they were stunned to see that the blade was untarnished despite having been soaked in underground water for centuries. The edge also still retained its sharpness, and was capable of cutting a stack of 20 pieces of paper.

The blade was largely made of copper which made it less likely to shatter, and the edge of the blade had more tin content which made the sword sharper, and sulfur was added to decrease the chance of tarnish in the patterns. This unique forge, along with the practically air-tight scabbard, is believed to explain why it was able to resist rusting for such a long period of time.

The sword blade is 55.7 cm in length and 4.6 cm wide, with a 8.4 cm long handle and weighs 936 grams. Each side of the blade is decorated with turquoise and one side of the blade, near the handle, has an inscription in an ancient Chinese script that says, *"Belonging to King Gou Jian of Yue, made for his personal use"*.

The weapon is considered a first level protected artifact of the People's Republic of China. The weapon is currently possessed by the Hubei Museum in the Hubei Province, China.

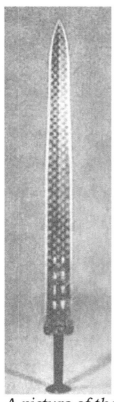

A picture of the Sword of Gou Jian. Taken from a Chinese high school textbook.

<u>Graban</u>: A sword forged by Ansias for Fortinbras (also known as 'Fierabras', or 'Strong-i-the-Arm' in some tales; the later is an English translation of what Fierabras means in French) from the Matter of France tales. Graban means 'Grave Digger'.

Source:
Song of Roland tales

<u>Grail, Holy</u>: A quite legendary chalice that is the subject of a wide range of stories from the medieval

age unto the present. The chalice is endowed with the power to preserve chastity and prolong life.

Legend has it the chalice is said to have gained its importance by having been the cup last drank from by Jesus Christ during the last supper, and later, in which Joseph of Arimathea caught the last drop of Christ's blood during his crucifixion.

Some stories say Joseph then brought the cup to England, while others say the Knights Templar found it during the Crusades and took it back among their riches.

The quest of the Holy Grail was the favorite subject of many medieval stories, particularly those pertaining to King Arthur's Knights of the Round Table. Each of the one hundred and fifty knights in King Arthur's court eventually would see the cup, but only the most pure hearted among them, Sir Galahad, was able to grasp hold of it.

Some stories describe the chalice as having been created from a single emerald.

Sources:
 'Encyclopaedia of Superstitions, Folklore and the Occult Sciences, Vol. II', by Cora Linn Daniels and C.M. Stevans, J.H. Yewdale and Sons Co. (1903)

<u>Grail Sword</u>: A sword that appears in various Arthurian tales surrounding the Grail 'Quests'. The Grail Sword has most to do with the quest of Sir Gawain, 'The Knight of the Goddess' and 'Hawk of May'.

In the tales, one of Sir Gawain's tasks is to first locate the broken 'Grail Sword' and return it back to the place it was forged. The Grail Sword, as it turns out, is actually the 'Sword of Light', 'The Sword of Naudu' (*see Claiomh Solais*), one of the Thirteen Treasures of Ireland but the story is odd in that the person who was suppose to have forged the sword was Wayland the Smith from Norse mythology, not Irish legends.

Despite this tidbit, in the tales Sir Gawain successfully locates the forge of Wayland and repairs the sword.

Other tales say that Sir Galahad, the son of Sir Lancelot of the Lake, is the one that re-forges the Grail Sword once he locates the Holy Grail. In it, Galahad uses the broken shards to detect the holy chalice, as the sword is a living thing and became healed once Galahad came close to the Grail.

The tales state that the sword was originally broken when it was used to murder a virtuous knight, though the identity of the knight tends to change from story to story.

Source:
Le Morte d'Arthur
Weston, Jessie Laidlay. *The Legend of Sir Perceval: Studies upon its Origin Development, and position in the Arthurian Cycle.* Published by David Nutt at the Sign of the Phoenix Long Acre. London 1906. Original from Stanford University

Gram: (Also known as "Balmung" in the *Nibelungenlied Saga*, and as Nothung in the *Die Walküre*), this is famously known as the magical sword of Sigurd (or Sigfried) Volsung (or Tarlung) from Norse mythology.

The name Gram name means 'grief'. It appears in the Volsunga Saga and Nibelungenlied poems, and was capable of cutting through any man-made object. It was regarded as one of the finest swords ever made, and became known as 'Fafnir's Bane'. Some said it was forged by Volund, and had the power to make the owner win all battles.

The story of Gram begins with a very strong sword carried by Odin into the hall of King Volsung of Hunland during a banquet celebrating the bequothment of King Volsung's daughter, Signy, to King Siggeir of Gautland. Odin brandished the sword before the party and thrust it into the 'Barnstock' (a mighty tree that grew in King Volsung's hall, also called 'Branstock') and announced to the startled crowd,

"He who draw this sword out of the trunk shall receive it from me as a gift, and he himself shall prove that he has never carried a better sword than this one." (Saga of the Volsungs, pg.3)

Odin then walked out of the hall as the nobles in the court rushed to the blade, and all of them attempted to pull it out. However, the only man who was able to withdraw the sword was Sigmund, the son of King Volsung. King Siggeir then offered Sigmund triple the sword's weight in gold if he would sell it to him, but the boy refused, saying that if the sword had been meant for the king it would have released itself to him instead.

King Siggeir was insulted by this, and began plotting Sigmund's demise. Three month's later, King Volsung and his three sons sailed to Gauteland at the invitation of King Siggeir, who had secretly gathered a large army to attack them when they came onshore. King Volsung was killed, and Sigmund eventually avenged his father by burning King Siggeir alive in his hall.

Sigmund returned to his country and assumed control of his father's lands and became a great king himself, and eventually married the daughter of King Eylimi, Hjordis. However, another suitor of Hjdoris, King Lyngvi, was jealous that Sigmund had been chosen and so he gathered an army to conquer Hunland.

In the battle, King Sigmund was mortally wounded when Gram broke against the spear of a foot soldier; who was actually Odin in disguise. The night after the battle, Hjordis came to him and Sigmund used his powers of prediction to give her a dying message;

"You are carrying a son. Raise him well and carefully, for he will be an excellent boy, the foremost of our line. Guard well the broken pieces of the sword. From them can be made a good sword, which will be called Gram. Our son will bear it and with it accomplish many great deeds, which will never be forgotten." (The Saga of the Volsungs, pg.54)

Hjdoris then married the Viking King Alf while she was still pregnant, but shortly then gave birth to Sigurd. Sigurd grew up and was loved by all, and was considered a talented warrior. Regin the dwarf (Mimir) became the boy's 'foster father', but Regin had a special plan for the boy, and eventually persuaded the boy that he could gain enough riches for himself to become a king if he slew the dragon Fafnir. Sigurd asked Regin to forge a sword for him that could kill the dragon, and the dwarf forged three fine swords—but Sigurd demanded a sword which could split an anvil in half, and broke each sword against an anvil when he test-cutted them.

Frustrated with Regin's craftsmanship, Sigurd collected the broken shards of Gram from his mother and asked Regin to form a sword that was "worthy of these fragments". The completed sword was wondrous;

"Now Regin made a sword. And when he brought it out of the forge, it seemed to the apprentices as if flames were leaping from its edges. He told Sigurd to take the sword and that he was no swordsmith if this one broke. Sigurd hewed at the anvil and split it to its base. The blade did not shatter or break. He praised the sword highly and went to the river with a tuft of wool, which he threw in against the current. The sword cut the wool in two when the tuft ran against the blade. Sigurd went home contented."
(Saga of the Volsungs, pg. 60)

Before going to slay Fafnir, Sigurd sets out to avenge his father's death. Using his mother's connections, he raises a large army then sets out to King Lyngvi's lands to conquer it. Wielding Gram, Sigurd slays hundreds of men (and even horses) in the resulting battle, cutting his way across the battlefield until he found King Lyngvi;

"So many fell from the ranks of the sons of Hunding that no one knew their number. And Sigurd was at the front of his troops. Then the sons of King Hunding attacked him. Sigurd struck at King Lyngvi and split his helmet and his head and his armored body. After that he cut Lyngvi's brother Hjorvard into two pieces. Then he killed the songs of Hunding who were still alive, along with the larger part of their army." (Saga of the Volsungs, pg 62)

Sigurd then keeps his promise to Regin and goes to slay Fafnir. Sigurd digs a ditch into the ground and waits at the den of Fafnir for the dragon to come out for water, and when he does, Sigurd thrusts the sword deep into Fafnir and gives him a mortal wound.

Sigurd then learns that Regin plans to betray him in order to get the gold all for himself, but having discovered the plot, the boy also slays Regin with the magic sword before Regin has a chance to kill Sigurd.

The later Nibelungenlied poems are a little different; Regin is the dragon and Mirmir is a separate person who is the foster-father of Sigurd.

The exact appearance of the weapon is obscure, but it was supposed to be a very large (seven 'hand spans' long) sword with a black handle, although the blade may have been refitted with gold decorations after Sigurd slew Fafnir, as a passage in the Saga of the Volsungs claims *"All Sigurd's weapons were ornamented with gold and were brown in color since he far surpassed other men in courtesy."*

What happened to the sword after Sigurd dies is unknown, for the rest of the Saga of the Volsungs doesn't mention it after Sigurd throws it to cut down Guttorm, the assasin who mortally wounds Sigurd in his sleep. However, it re-appears later in the Thidrekssaga (1250), in the hands of Hildebrand (Hildibrandr).

However, in the Thdreskssaga, Rodingeir receives Gram from King Gunner ('Gunther', German) of Burgundy during the wedding of King Attila of the Huns and Grimhild, a Burgundian princess.

The sword 'Mimung' in the Thdreskssaga is somewhat based on, but is not the same sword, as Gram appears as a separate weapon in it.

Sources:
Saga of the Volsungs
Der Ring des Nibelungen: Die Walküre, an opera by Richard Wagner (1856)

<u>Grid's Rod</u>: An iron staff given to Thor so he could kill the Troll King.

<u>Green Dragon Crescent Blade</u>: Also known as the 'Blue Dragon' or 'Frost Blade', this was a 'kwan dao' (a cross between a Chinese saber and a

polearm, a similar concept to a glaive) that belonged to the legendary Chinese hero, General Guan Yu. The Green Dragon Crescent Blade weighs approximately 100 pounds.

The names 'Blue Dragon' and 'Frost Blade' come from a story where during a battle in snow, the blade of the weapon became covered in blood. The blood then froze and created a layer of frost on the blade.

Chinese myth says that Guan Yu invented the Kwan Dao and had the Green Dragon Crescent Blade forged. If this were true, then the Green Dragon Crescent Blade would be the first Kwan Dao ever forged.

The weapon is currently on display at the ancient Purple Cloud Temple in Wudangshan, China.

Source:
Luó Guànzhōng. *Romance of the Three Kingdoms*.

Great Sword of State, The: One of the three "Swords of Justice" of British coronation regalia. It is a large 47 ½ inch two-handed sword that weighs eight pounds.

The sword represents the sovereign's power and authority, and it is carried before the sovereign on all state occasions.

Greysteel: The sword of Kol the Thrall. The Dwarves forged the sword so that "no spells could deaden its edge, and it would bite whatsoever it fell on, whether iron or aught else."

Kol lent the sword to Gisli to slay Bjorn the "Bearsark" (Berserker) but when it was time for Gisli to return the sword, Gisli instead killed Kol with it. However, Kol laid a curse upon Gisli and the sword as Greysteel's blade shattered on Kol's head,

"It had been better now that I had got back my sword when I asked for it; and yet this is but the beginning of the ill luck which it will bring on thy kith and kin."

Gisli had the pieces re-forged by Thorgrim into a spear which Gisli then used in many adventures, but wherever Gisli went ill-luck traveled with him.

Source:
The Gentleman's Magazine and Historical Review, Vol. II, July-Dec, 1866. Bradbury, Evans & Co, 11 Bouverie Street, London

Gisli Saga

<u>Grus</u>: The sword of Duke Boleslaw III Krzywousty (1085 – 1138) of Poland.

Boleslaw III Wrymouth. Drawing by Jan Matejko.

<u>Gungnir:</u> (Also spelled Gungni Gungner and Gungrir) The spear of Odin, the chief god of Norse mythology and paganism. The name means "The Swaying One".

It was forged by the dwarf Dvalin. The spear has the unique characteristic of always hitting its target, and when thrown will always return to the hand of the one who threw it.

H

<u>Hades, Helmet of:</u> The helmet of the Greek god Hades, given to Perseus so he could slay Medusa. It made the wearer invisible.

Sources
Encyclopedia of Mythology, Arthur Cotterell

<u>Hand of Glory:</u> A magical item common to superstitious tales in France, Germany and Spain.

A hand of glory is created from the hand of a hanged man that had been pickled with saltpeter, salt and pepper after having the blood squeezed out with a winding sheet. The hand was then made to hold a candle molded from the fat of the hanged man, virgin wax, and sesame of Lapland. When lit, the candle had the power to stupify people and render them incapacitated. It was believed to be popular among burglars and assassins.

Another variation on the creation of a hand of glory was by ransacking the grave of an unborn child, removing the hand, and then nailing it to the door of the house that the robbers intended to burglarize. So long as the hand was nailed to the door, all of the occupants within would remain asleep.

Sources:

'Encyclopaedia of Superstitions, Folklore and the Occult Sciences, Vol. II', by Cora Linn Daniels and C.M. Stevans, J.H. Yewdale and Sons Co. (1903)

Hanjo Masamune: A legendary sword that was the symbol of the Tokugawa Shogunate. Also spelled as 'Honjo Masamune'. *See "Masamune swords".*

Harmonia, Necklace of: A necklace forged by Hephaistos for Harmonia, the child of Ares and Aphrodite. Harmonia (Concordia to the Romans) was the Greek goddess of harmony and concord and child of Aphrodite and Ares by infidelity.

Hephaestus, blacksmith of the Olympian gods, discovered his wife, Aphrodite, goddess of love, having a sexual affair with Ares, the god of war. He became enraged and vowed to avenge himself for Aphrodite's infidelity by cursing any lineage of children resulting from the affair. Aphrodite ended up bearing Ares a daughter, Harmonia. The girl was was later betrothed to Cadmus of Thebes. Upon hearing of the royal engagement, Hephaestus presented Harmonia with the necklace as a wedding gift, yet unbeknownst to her it had been secretly cursed to bring misfortune to her.

The magical necklace allowed any woman wearing it to remain eternally young and beautiful. It thus became a much-coveted object amongst women of the House of Thebes. Although no solid description of the Necklace exists, it is usually described in ancient Greek passages as being of beautifully wrought gold, in the shape of two serpents whose open mouths formed a clasp, and inlaid with various jewels.

Hatf
(Also called Halef) One of the nine swords of the prophet Muhammad of Islamic legend. Hatf was a sword that Muhammad took as booty from the Banu Qaynaqa. Its name means "the deadly".

Legend has it that King David forged the sword after God gave him the ability to work with iron to forge weapons and armor. The Hatf resembled the al-Battar, but is larger than it.

King David was said to have passed the sword onto the tribe of the Levites who kept the weapons of the Israelites until Muhammad claimed it.

A relic said to be the sword is currently housed in the Topkapi Museum in Istanbul.

Hauteclere
(Also spelled Haute-Clair, or Altachiara) The sword of Oliver (Olivier or Closamont), one of the Twelve Paladins (peers) of Charlemagne from medieval European legends. Its name means 'very bright' or 'glorious'. The sword was very powerful, and in one tale, it shattered the nine magical blades forged by the smiths Munifician, Ansias, and Galas.

In the Gerard de Vienne (Gautier), the blade of the weapon was described as being forged from a very brownish steel that was described as "rough", and that it had a crystal embedded in its golden hilt.

"Where is your sword, that Halteclere I knew?

Golden its hilt, whereon a crystal grew"

In the Croquemitaine (1863) by Enerest L'Epine (pen name Quatrelle), Hauteclere appears under the name 'Glorious' and Hauteclaire is a different sword wielded by a knight named Closamont—a new character.

In the tale, Oliver is able to shatter the swords Baptism, Florece, Graban, Flamberge, Joyeuse, Hauteclaire, Durandal, Sauvagins and Cortain.

However, in the poem 'La Mariage de Roland' by Victor Hugo, Closamont was the name given for Oliver's sword, so it would appear that Ernest had become confused about the names when he wrote Croquemitaine.

In some Italian tales, the sword was called 'Altachiara' and had previously been the sword of Lancelot.

Sources:
Croquemitaine
La Mariage de Roland

Heracles, Bow of:

No one but Heracles' friend Philoctetes (in some versions: Iolaus or Poeas) would light his funeral pyre. For this action, Philoctetes (or Poeas) received Heracles' bow and arrows, which were later needed by the Greeks to defeat Troy in the Trojan War. Philoctetes confronted Paris and shot a poisoned arrow at him. The Hydra poison would subsequently lead to the death of Paris. The

Trojan War, however, would continue until the Trojan Horse was used to defeat Troy.

"Over his shoulders the fierce warrior put the steel that saves men from doom, and across his breast he slung behind him a hollow quiver. Within it were many chilling arrows, dealers of death which makes speech forgotten: in front they had death, and trickled with tears; their shafts were smooth and very long; and their butts were covered with feathers of a brown eagle." Hesiod, The Shield of Heracles 122-327

The richly decorated quiver of Herakles was crafted by Hephaistos. Philoktetes possessed it and the hero's bow at the time of the Trojan War.

Heracles, Club of: The Greek hero Heracles used this club to defeat the magical Nemean lion creature that could not be harmed by arrows as the first of his labors.

Heracles, Cup of: An amethyst cup owned by Heracles, one of the female descendants of the invincible Greek hero Hercules. The cup protected her from the effects of poison, pain, disease and plague. It was given to her by a stork.

Sources:
 'Encyclopaedia of Superstitions, Folklore and the Occult Sciences, Vol. II', J.H. Yewdale and Sons Co. (1903)

Hippolyta, Girdle of: The magic girdle of Hippolyta, a Queen of the Amazons in Greek mythology. The girdle had been given to her by her father, Ares the God of War, and was a symbol of her authority as queen. It was also known as the belt of Ares, zoster, and it was probably more of heavy warrior's belt than a girdle. The belt symbolised her power as leader of the Amazon tribes.

Obtaining the girdle was the subject of one of Heracles labors. Admeta, daughter of Eurystheus, wanted this belt so badly that the Mycenaean king sent Heracles to fetch the belt for his ninth labour. In most version, Heracles killed the queen and took the belt from her. But in one version, Heracles captured Melanippe, and ransomed the Amazon commander for the belt.

Hofud: The so-called 'sword' of Heimdall, a Norse god. Heimdall was the guardian of Bifrost.

Although it is often called a sword, Hofud is usually spoken of as if it was a helmet with dagger-like horns stemming from it, sort of like the horns of a ram.

Source:
Dumézil, Georges (1959). "Comparative Remarks on the Scandinavian God Heimdall", *Gods of the Ancient Northmen*. Ed. Einar Haugen, trans. Francis Charat (1973). Berkeley: University of California Press. ISBN 0-520-03507-0.

Holy Spear: *See 'Longinus, Lance of'.*

Holyrood: The Holyrood or Holy Rood is a Christian relic considered to be part of the **True Cross** on which Jesus died. The word derives from the Old English *rood*, meaning a cross, or from the Scots *haly ruid* ("holy cross"). Several relics venerated as part of the True Cross are known by this name, in England, Ireland and Scotland.

Honoree: A sword from Arthurian myths and legends that could only be withdrawn from its scabbard by the son of Gwalchmei, Biausdous. By unsheathing Honoree, Biausdous earned the right to marry Biautei, daughter of the King of the Isles.

Gwalchmei was the forerunner of Gawain, though some think he is the same character as Eliwlod. (more research needed)

Source:
Encyclopedia of the Celts

Horus, Staff of: A falcon headed staff

Hrungnir, Shield of: In Norse mythology, a stone shield owned by the frost giant Hrungnir. Because his head, heart and shield were made of stone, Thor, the god of thunder, needed to use his magical hammer Mjonlinir to defeat him.

Sources:
Encyclopedia of Mythology, Arthur Cotterell

Hrunting: A magic sword that appears in the Old English epic 'Beowulf' and John C. Gardner's

'Grendel'. The sword was supposed to possess great power, but it proved ineffective against Grendel's mother.

"That sword was called Hrunting,
an ancient heritage:
Steel was the blade itself,
tempered with poison-twigs,
Hardened with battle-blood:
never in fight it failed
Any who wielded it,
when he would wage a strife
In the dire battlefield,
folk-moot of enemies."

Beowulf was lent the sword by Unferth, a baron in the court of the King Hrothar of Denmark, after the sword had been used to slice Grendel's arm.

However, Beowulf was unable to use the sword during the battle, and ended up using a different sword he found inside the monster's lair—one that had belonged to the giant race of Jotuns.

"So he gazed at the walls,
saw there a glorious sword,
An old brand gigantic,
trusty in point and edge,
An heirloom of heroes;
that was the best of blades,
Splendid and stately,
the forging of giants;
but it was huger than,
any of human race
Could bear to battle-strife,

save Beowulf only."

Beowulf used the Jotun's sword to decapitate the monster, but her blood was acidic and melted the blade.

Hymir, Cauldron of: In Norse mythology, the mile-wide cauldron owned by Hymir, a frost giant and father of the war god Tyr. The cauldron was enormous and was able to brew ale for all of the gods.

Sources:
Encyclopedia of Mythology, Arthur Cotterell

I

<u>Ice-brook</u>: (Sword of Spain, the Isebrookes templer) The sword of Othello from the Shakespearean play of the same name.

The sword received its name, apparently, from being quenched in a cold brook after it was tempered.

Source:
Othello, William Shakespear

<u>Ilya Muromets, Imperishable Relic of Saint:</u>
The purported remains of Ilya Muromet.

Ilya Muromets is a Russian folk epic hero. He is the only epic hero made a saint by the Russian Orthodox Church. He was a bogatyr, a kind of Russian knight errant. His remains are said to be held at the Caves of Saint Anthony at Kiev Pechersk Lavra, Ukraine.

<u>Invisibility, Ring of</u>: Given to Sir Owain, one of King Arthur's knights. The ring was given to him by a woman named Luned so he could hide from the Black Knight he had fatalled wounded, until the knight died. With Luned's help, Owain convinced the Black Knight's widow to marry him, thus Sir Owan became the master of the Castle of the Fountain, the Black Knight's stronghold.

Source:
Encyclopedia of Mythology, Arthur Cotterell

J

<u>Jagdamba</u>: One of the swords owned by Chhatrapati Shivaji (April 6, 1630 C.E.- April 3, 1680 C.E.), Emperor and High Protector of the Maratha Empire. In India, the stories of Shivaji have become legendary and he is considered a folk hero.

Emperor Shivaji was known to possess three sword; Bhawani, Jagdamba and Tulja. Jagdamba was gifted to Prince Edward VII of Wales. The sword is kept in Buckingham Palace in London.

Bhawani was said to have been made forged in Toledo, Spain. It is believed to be in the hands of Udayraje Bhosale of Satara who is a direct descendent of Shivaji. However, the sword is engaved with the name "Shahu Chhatrapati". This causes some scholars to doubt its authenticity.

As for Tulja, the sword has been lost for centuries.

<u>Jamshid, Cup of</u>: A cup of divination featured in Persian mythology. The cup has also been called *Jam-e Jahan nama, Jam-e Jahan Ara, Jam-e Giti nama*, and **Jam-e Kei-khosrow**. It is the subject of many Persian poems and stories.

It was long possessed by rulers of ancient Persia and was said to be filled with an elixir of immortality. The whole world was said to be reflected in it.

Divinations within the cup were said to reveal deep truths. Sometimes, especially in popular depictions such as The Heroic Legend of Arslan, the cup has been visualized as a crystal ball. Helen Zimmern's English translation of the Shahnameh uses the term "crystal globe"

Jan III, Sword of: Sword of King Jan Sobieski III (17 August 1629 C.E. - 17 June 1696 C.E.: also known as *John III Sobieski*).

The sword was given to King Jan III in the cathedral in Żółkiew, Ukraine in 1684 C.E., as a sign of gratitude for his protection of the Church against the Turks.

The sword was forged in Rome in 1676. It has a steel blade that is partly gilded; bearing an inscription that refers to Pope Innocent XI. The hilt is gilded silver and the highly decorated sheath bears a coat of arms belonging to Clemens X.

The sword was kept by the Radziwiłł family in Nieśwież until it was looted by the Russians in 1812 C.E.. The sword was then donated to the collection in Carskie Sioło, and then to the Hermitage collection in St. Petersburg. It was recovered by Poland in 1924 C.E. and finally donated to the Wawel Royal Castle National Art Collection.

Sword of King Jan Sobieski III

Source:
Wawel Royal Castle National Art Collection

<u>Jesus, Sandals of:</u> The remains of an ornate fabric slipper allegedly from the Merovingian period (fifth to eighth centuries AD), which were given to the Abbey of Prüm of by Rome in the Carolingian period (seventh to ninth centuries).

The sandals were among the most important relics of the **Catholic Church** in Middle Ages. The sandals are pointed out by King Pepin III within the deed of 762, where it is mentioned Pepin received them as a present from Pope Zachary (741-752) and Pope Stephen II (752-757); Pope Zachary had recognized Pepin's election as king and Pope Stephen II completed the present in 754.

Aside from its religious significance, the relic was physical proof that the Frankish king's right to rule had been acknowledged by Rome.

Jesus, Seamless Robe of:
Also known as the Holy Robe, the Holy Tunic, the Honorable Robe, and the Chiton of the Lord.

In the 12th Century the **Roman Catholic Diocese of Trier** claimed to possess the seamless robe of Jesus, and thus became a more popular destination for pilgrimage than the Abbey of **Prüm** (which possessed the so-called Sandals of Jesus).

Source:
Relics of the Christ. Nickell, Joe (2007). University Press of Kentucky. p. 104. ISBN 0-8131-2425-5.

Jeweled Sword of Offering:
Also known as the Jeweled State Sword, it was the Sword of King George IV of the United Kingdom of Great Britain and Ireland which existed from 1820-1930 C.E. The sword was forged for his coronation ceremony, and has been used in such ceremonies (including knighting ceremonies) by the British royal family ever since.

The blade of the sword is damask steel and kept in a gold scabbard set with jewels of every color that compose various images such as an English rose, Scottish thistle and an Iris shamrock.

Some view the weapon as being the most beautiful and valuable sword in the world. It is one of the three "Swords of Justice" of British coronation regalia.

Joan, Sword of: The sword of Joan of Arc, also named Jeanne d'Arc and Jeanne la Pucelle ("Joan the Virgin"). Some legends say Charles Martel (who defeated the Umayyad at the Battle of Tours in 732 C.E and was the grandfather of Charlemagne) once wielded the blade, while others say the sword was sent to her by God. Some legends go further and say that both cases are true.

During her trial, the judges asked Joan about the sword. It is recorded that Joan had sent a letter to the clergy of the Church of Saint Catherine de Fierbois asking for a sword that lay buried behind the altar of the chapel. When the clergy searched, a rusty sword was found and sent to her. When Joan was asked how she knew the sword would be there, Joan replied that the voices of Arch-angel Michael, Saint Catherine of Alexandria and Saint Margaret of Antioch had told her in a vision.

From the court records,

"Whilst I was at Tours, or at Chinon, I sent to seek for a sword which was in the Church of Saint Catherine de Fierbois, behind the altar; it was found there at once; the sword was in the ground, and rusty; upon it were five crosses; I knew by my Voice where it was...It was under the earth, not very deeply buried, behind the altar, so it seemed to me: I do not know exactly if it were before or behind the altar, but I believe I wrote saying that it was at the back. As soon as it was found, the Priests of the

Church rubbed it, and the rust fell off at once without effort. It was an armorer of Tours who went to look for it. The Priests of Fierbois made me a present of a scabbard; those of Tours, of another; one was of crimson velvet, the other of cloth-of-gold. I had a third made of leather, very strong. When I was taken prisoner I had not got this sword. I always bore the sword of Fierbois from the time I had it up to my departure from Saint-Denis, after the attack on Paris."

Three stories exist for how the sword came to be buried in the church.

1. Charles Martel had founded the Church of Saint Catherine de Fierbois and, at the advice of the Christian God, buried his sword there for the next person who would be chosen to defend France from invasion.
2. Charles Martel founded the Church and, after his victory at Tours, buried the sword as an offering to God and Saint Catherine.
3. The Christian God put the sword into the ground for Joan to claim.

An alternate theory suggests the sword was one of the many such weapons of armament left by pilgrimaging knights who had visited the chapel.

Based upon Joan's own testimony, the only thing known about the description of the sword is that it had five crosses on it.

As for what happened to the sword, those details were not recorded. When Joan was inquired about it at her trial, she had only this to say,

"To tell what became of the sword does not concern this Case, and I will not answer about it now. My brothers have all my goods – my horses, my sword, so far as I know, and the rest, which are worth more than twelve thousand crowns."

Image of Joan of Arc painted between 1450 C.E. and 1500 C.E.

Sources:
Jeanne D'Arc, Maid of Orleans, 1429-1431, T. Douglas Murray ed., McClure, Phillips & Co., New York, 1902. pp 27-30.

Joyeuse: Also called 'Fusberta Joyosa, this was the sword of Charlemagne (742 C.E. – 28 January 814 C.E.), King of the Franks and Emperor of the Romans. The name Joyeuse means "joyful". It was said to be able to emit a light wave that could slice the tops off a hill and grant the wielder immunity to all poisons. The sword was forged by Galas.

Some legends say its pommel was forged from the Lance of Longinus, while others say it was smithed from the same materials as Durandel and Curtana (*See "Durandel" and "Curtana"*).

The sword is described in The Song of Roland, an 11th century poem:

"Charlemagne was wearing his fine white coat of mail and his helmet with gold-studded stones; by his side hung Joyeuse, and never was there a sword to match it; its color changed thirty times a day."

The sword was said to be buried with Charlemagne when he died, although there is two actual swords which both claim to be Joyeuse: one is held by the Louvre and was used in the coronation of French kings, while the other is held at the Imperial Treasury in Vienna.

A portrait of Charlemagne by Albrecht Dürer that was painted several centuries after Charlemagne's death.

Judas Maccabeus, gold sword of:
In Hebrew mythology, this is the sword that Judas saw when Jeremiah, a prophet of God, sent him a vision.

"Whereupon Jeremias holding forth his right hand gave to Judas a sword of gold, and in giving it spake thus,

Take this holy sword, a gift from God, and with the which thou shall wound the adversaries."

However, the image of the sword seemed to be a spiritual message, as Judas wake up and the sword was nowhere to be found.

Source:
2 Maccabees 15:12-16

Justice, Sword of: Sword of Justitia, the Roman Goddess of Justice. Images of Justitia are popular all over the world, and frequently adorn courtrooms. In some cultures she is known as 'Lady Justice'.

Since the Renaissance, Justitia has been depicted as a woman carrying a sword and scales while wearing a blindfold. The blindfold she wears represents that justice should be dealt out objectively, without fear or favor, regardless of the identity of the individual on trial. The scale she carries in her left hand is used to measure the strength of a case's support and opposition.

The double-edged Sword of Justice that she carries in her right hand symbolizes punishment, and is a throwback to the executioner's sword for carrying out capital punishment.

Lady Justice Standing

K

<u>Karsnaut:</u> A sword from the Scandinavian Grettis Saga, used by the anti-hero Grettir Ásmundarson, also known as Grettir the Strong. Karsnaut is the sword he wielded in his last battle.

"Then they laid open the end of one of the timbers and bore upon it until it broke. Grettir was unable to rise from his knees, but he seized the sword Karsnaut at the moment when they all sprang in from the roof, and a mighty fray began. Grettir struck with his sword at Vikar, a man of Hjalti the son of Thord, reaching his left shoulder as he sprang from the roof. It passed across his shoulder, out under his right arm, and cut him right in two. His body fell in two parts on the top of Grettir and prevented him from recovering his sword as quickly as he wished, so that Thorbjorn Angle was able to wound him severely between the shoulders. Grettir said: "Bare is his back who has no brother!""

Karsnaut is another example of the demon-exorcising sword motif found in Germanic stories, such as Beowulf. Kaursnat was won by Grettir when he defeated Kar the Old (a haugr, or howe revenant) in his grave mound.

Grettir also owned the swords Aettartangi (translated as 'tang' or 'hilt of the generations'; also known in the saga as Jokulsnautr, the Gift of Jokull, a sword which also appears in the

Vatnsdaela Saga). Aettartangi had been given to him by his mother Asdis.

Kavacha: Magical golden armor that belonged to Karna, one of the important characters of the *'Mahābhārata'*, from Hindu mythology.

Karna was the son of the sun god Surya, conceived by his mother Kunti. Karna was the result of an immaculate conception, and was born with armor and earrings apart of his body. So long as he wore the armor, Kavacha, and the earrings, Kundala, the boy would be invincible.

When Karna became the king of Anga, he pledged that anyone he would honor the request of anyone who approached him during his Sun worshiping ceremonies. This oath later came into play against him when Karna was preparing to battle against the Pandavas in the Kurukshetra War. Indra, the king of the Gods was worried, as his son Indra was fated to battle against Karna. Indra decided to take the form of a beggar and approach Karna during midday worship, and requests his armor. Karna then cuts his armor off his body to honor his oath. Feeling ashamed for using deceipt, Indra teaches Karna the invocation for Indra's most powerful celestial weapon, the 'Vasavi shakti', but tells Karna he will only be allowed to use it once.

Unfortunately for Karna, he would never have the chance to use this weapon in battle. Before the war, Karna promises his mother he will not use a divine weapon more than once. As Karna already possessed the ability to use the 'Nagastra' divine weapon, he chose to invoke this weapon against Arjuna in battle, but missed, and thus was unable to attack Arjuna again. Karna was thus defeated by Arjuna.

See '*Astra*' for more information.

Sources:
'*Mahābhārata*'

<u>Kladenets:</u> A magical sword from Slavic mythology. It appears in a wide variety of Russian fairytales. In "The Tale about the City of Babylon" it is called "Asp the Serpent". In the "Tale about bogatyr Yeruslan Lazarevich" it is mentioned amonf the fire shield and fire spear.

The name Kladenets appears to be derived from the Slavic word for treasure, but Max Vasmer theorized that it may have originated as a corruption of the pronouncation of Clarent. (See Clarent). It is also similar to the verb "klast" (to put down in Russian) so it may correspond to "slayer" in English.

<u>Knots:</u> Knots were viewed as possessing supernatural importance.

Before a child was born, it was common for a midwife to untie all knots and unlock every door in a house, with the belief that tied knots or locks could cause a baby to become stillborn if they were enchanted by a malicious witch.

Sources
Encyclopedia of Supersitions

<u>Koh-i-noor</u>: or the "Mountain of Light", also known as "The Great Mogul" is a rather famous diamond. For centuries the Koh-i-noor has been the talisman of India. It is believed that any water the diamond is dipped into will become enchanted, capable of curing all diseases.

In the forteenth century it was held by the rajah of Malwa. Later it fell into the hands of the sultans of Delhi, after their conquest of Malwa. It belonged in the seventeenth century to Aurungzebe the Great. The shah Jihan sent it to Hortensio Borgio to be cut, but the Venetian lapidary reduced it from '793 5/8 carats to 186, leaving it dull and lusterless. It next passed into the hands of Aurungzebe's great grandson, who it in his turban. Nadir Shah invited him to a feast and insisted on changing turbans "to cement their love", thus it fell into the hands of Nadir, who gave it the name "Koh-i-noor".

The diamond then passed to Ahmed Shah, the founder of the Cabul dynasty; was extorted from Shah Shuja by by Runjeet Singh, who wore it set in a bracelet. After the murder of Shu Singh, it was deposited into the Lahore Treasury and after the annexation of the Punjaub, was presented to Queen Victoria in 1849. It was then re-cut, reducing it to 106 carats.

There is another diamond of the same name in the possession of the Shah of Persia.

Sources:

'Encyclopaedia of Superstitions, Folklore and the Occult Sciences, Vol. II', by Cora Linn Daniels and C.M. Stevans, J.H. Yewdale and Sons Co. (1903)

Kolebrand: Sword of Sir Ribolt, it was also known as "Coalbrand". It comes from the Danish ballad "Ribolt's fight with the dragon and Aller", a ballad from the Faroe Islands in Northern Europe. The song is sometimes known as "I see so Many Man-of-Wars".

"Sir Ribolt stamp'd on the hill so hard,
While his steel-spit brandish'd he :
' Give me out Coalbrand the good sword,
Or I'll have a tuzzle with thee.'"
' Thou shalt not get Coalbrand to-day,
The sword so lov'd by me ;
It never shall come into thy hand,
Whilst life in my body be.'
They fought for a day, and for two they fought;
As the third day to evening drew,
Sir Ribolt struck so manfully
That the Dragon he overthrew."

Sources:
Ribolt's fight with the dragon and Aller, A Traditional Danish Ballad

Kongō, A trident-shaped staff which emits a bright light in the darkness. It gives a man wisdom and insight. The staff belonged originally to the Japanese mountain-god Koya-no-Myoin. It is the equivalent of the Sanskrit vajra, the lightning-jewel of the mountain-god Indra. There the staff represents the three flames of the sacrificial fire, part of the image of the vajra wheel.

Kusanagi-no-tsrurugi

A legendary sword of Japanese myth. Its name means either 'Grass Cutter' or 'Sword of snakes'. Its original name was "Ame no Murakumo no Tsurugi", which means "Sword of the heaven of the clustering clouds" or "Sword of the Billowing Clouds". If Excalibur can be considered the most legendary sword in British mythology, then Kusanagi is the most legendary sword of Japanese mythology.

The sword was said to have been discovered by the sea god Susanoo inside the fourth tail of a monstrous eight-headed snake demon, the Yamato no Orochi ("big snake of eight branches"). The story goes that while traveling, Susanoo encountered the elder of a grieving family. When Susanoo asked the elder what was wrong, the old man told the god that a fearsome serpent had consumed seven of his eight daughters and the creature was coming for his final daughter, Kushi-Nada-Hime. Susanoo promised to defeat the serpent in exchange for the Kushi's hand in marriage, which the elder accepted.

Susanoo then set eight vats of sake to be put on individual platforms positioned behind a fence with eight gates. When the Orochi came to the elder's house, the monster stuck its eight heads through the gates and drank the sake. Susanoo then attacked, swiftly decapitating each head of the monster. Susanoo then proceeded to cut the rest of the serpent's body into small pieces but in the fourth tail, Susanoo discovered a great sword hidden inside the body and named it "Ame no Murakumo no Tsurugi".

Susanoo then gave the sword to his sister, the sun goddess Amaterasu. Amaterasu passed the sword down to her human descendents, the Japanese Imperial family, as proof of their divine right to rule.

In addition to the mirror Yata no Kagami and Magatama sacred jewels, the Kusanagi sword composed of the "Three Imperial Treasures" of Japan. The sword represented the virtue of "Valor".

A popular tale on how the sword gained a second name relates a story from when the sword came into the hands of Prince Yamato Takeru, son of 12th Emperor Keiko. Takeru was once caught in a trap by a warlord who attempted to burn him to death by igniting a field around the boy. The prince swung the sword around him in an attempt to cut the roots of the grass around him but discovered that each sword swing caused him to shift the winds in the direction of the blow. Takeru used this magical power to redirect the blazing fires back upon the warlord and his men. The prince renamed the sword Kusanagi-no-tsrurugi "Grass Cutter" after this incident.

Although this tale is popular, some scholars of ancient Japanese linguistics disagree point out that in the original Japanese language of the time, "kusa" meant sword and "nagi" meant snake. The sword was most likely called "Sword of the Snake" because it was pulled out from the body of a giant snake monster.

The Kusanagi is frequently represented in literature and art as a curved, single-edged katana; however, if it really existed, it would have actually been a bronze-age sword, double-edged and straight.

According to the Nihon Shoki (a historical document of Japan) the sword was removed from the Imperial palace in 688 C.E. and enshrined in the Atsuta Shrine. However, another popular legend says that the sword was lost in 1185 C.E. during the Battle of Dannoura when the child Emperor Antoku committed suicide in the waters of the strait with the three imperial treasures. Though the Yata no Kagami and Magatama were recovered, according to this story the Kusanagi was not reclaimed.

Some sources claim that the Emperor Sujin ordered the fashioning of a replica of Kusanagi and it is this replica that is currently housed in the Atsuta Shrine.

Sources:

Kojiki ("Records of Ancient Matters")
Nihon Shoki ("The Chronicles of Japan")

L

<u>Laevateinn</u>: An extremely powerful flaming sword wielded by Surtr (Surtur, Surt), leader of the fire giants, at Ragnarok (End of the Gods) in Norse mythology. It was known as 'The Sword of Revenge'. The sword was forged by Volund.

At the battle of Ragnarok, Sutr engages the unarmed god Freyr in battle and quickly slays him with it. (See 'Freyr's Sword')

'In Surtr's grasp, the Sword of Revenge blazes, adding a blood red color to the twilight of the whole world'—which essentially means Laevateinn will engulf the world in fires that turn it into a volcanic, desolate wasteland. The only humans that survive the aftermath are those that will take shelter in the Ygdrassil (The World Tree).

The legend of the sword Laevateinn is possibly connected to Christian mythology of the 'Leviathan' monster that is supposed to appear during the 'Apocalypse'—the Christian 'End of the World' myth. However, the similarities may be pure coincidence.

"The Giant with the Flaming Sword", illustration by John Charles Dollman (1851-1934)

Sources:
Svipdagsmal

Sources:
'*Encyclopaedia of Superstitions, Folklore and the Occult Sciences, Vol. II*', by Cora Linn Daniels and C.M. Stevans, J.H. Yewdale and Sons Co. (1903)

Ladder, Jackob's: From the Biblical story described in the book of Genesis. Angels walked up and down it at the same time. It was described as a stairwell leading to the heavens.

Leochain: One of the swords of Fergus Mac Roich, the former king of Ulster during the stories contained in the Ulster Cycle of Irish mythology. Leochain was one of two swords belonging to Fergus, the other being the far more famous Caladbolg (*See Caladbolg*).

Sources:
Ulster Cycle

Life-Stone: An amulet worn by Bersi in the Icelandic story Kormaks Saga. Bersi and Steinia were in a swimming competition. Steina, knowing that Bersi wore the amulet to protect himself from injury, swam up to his competitor and tore the amulet from his neck, casting it off into the sea. It was found in the ebb tide by Thord, who being an enemy of Bersi, kept possession of it, but when Bersi was wounded, Thord returned the amulet and thus Bersi was healed.

Sources:
'Encyclopaedia of Superstitions, Folklore and the Occult Sciences, Vol. II', by Cora Linn Daniels and C.M. Stevans, J.H. Yewdale and Sons Co. (1903)

Lightning Flash: The Sword of God from Hebrew mythology, Lightning Flash is the name given to the flaming sword wielded by the angel who guards the Gates to Eden in Genesis 3:24.

According to Hebrew mythologies (and their derivites, such as Christianity), an angel armed with the Lightning Flash was placed by God at the Gates of Paradise after Adam and Eve, the first humans, were banished from God's grace. The angel's purpose is to prevent humans from ever entering

Paradise again, although some Christian denominations say the guard was removed when Jesus of Narzareth was born..

"After he drove the man out, he placed on the east side of the Garden of Eden cherubim and a flaming sword flashing back and forth to guard the way to the tree of life."

The Lighting Flash is also a symbol in Kabbalah made by connecting the Ten Sephiroth of Life in their numerical order. Kabballistic theory envisions the Lightning Flash as representative of the descent of creative power down the Planes of Being at the beginning of the universe.

Source:
Genesis 3:24, New International Version
The New Encyclopedia of the Occult, John Michael Greer, Llewellyn Publications (2003)

<u>Lobera</u>: Sword of Ferdinand III, King of Castile, and King of Leon. According to Don Juan Manual, Duke of Penafiel, in his Book of the examples of Count Lucanor and of Patrinio (published in 1337), Lobera had been the sword of Fernan Gonzalez, an epic hero who had been the first count of Castille.

Lobera was forged in steel, has a blade of 80 cm. With silver oranaments. It is a relic kept in the Capilla Real at the Seville Cathedral.

Instead of the more traditional rod, Ferdinand used a sword as a symbol of power.

Logthe: Sword of the son of Ole Siward, the King of the Goths.

Source:
Saxo Grammaticus, The Danish History, Books I-IX

Longinus, Lance of: Also called The Spear of Destiny, The Holy Lance, Spear of Longinus, or Holy Spear. An artifact said to be the spear which a Roman soldier used to pierce the side of Jesus Christ while he was crucified.

The spear is named after the Roman soldier Longinus, who was named in the Gospel of Nicodemus.

Through history, several objects have claimed to be the lance. In 1098, a Crusader named Peter Bartholomew unearthed a spear in St. Peter's Cathedral in Antioch which he claimed to be Longinus. Peter claimed he was led to the spear by a vision from St. Andrew. This lance is currently in Atschmiadzin, but it apparently is not a Roman lance at all, but the head of a flagpole.

The Vatican also holds a lance that is purported to be Longinus. This relic is located in St Peter's Basilica in Rome.

Source: Gospel of (John 19:31-37)

Luin: Also called Luisne, Brionac and the Spear of Lugh. This is the spear of the god Lugh. The spear is one of the Four Hallows of Ireland. The name means 'flaming' or 'glaring'.

It was originally forged by the Smith of Falias to be used against Balor of the Evil Eye, though in some stories the spear accompanied Lugh from the "otherworld" that the Tuatha De' Danann came from.

The spear was ascribed several powers:

1. Its blade burned so got that it had to be kept point-down in a barrel of water when not used in battle.

2. It constantly dripped blood.

3. Whoever wielded it in battle would emerge victorious.

Sources:
'The Hisory of Ireland', Keating, Geoffrey.

Lu Tung Pin, Sword of: The unnamed magical sword wielded by the deity Lu Tung Pin (also known as Lǚ Dòngbīn), leader of the "Eight Immortals" and hero of early Chinese literature. Revered by Daoists, Lu Tung Pin is the object of several tales detailing his life of renouncing riches, punishing the wicked, rewarding the good, and slaying dragons with his sword that can dispel evil.

Lyusing: One of the two swords that belonged to Ragnald of Norway. The other was Whitting. (*See Whitting*)

Source:

Saxo Grammaticus, The Danish History, Books I-IX

M

Mac an Luin: Sword of Finn Mac Cumaill (also known as "Finn Maccumhail", "mac Umaill", "Fingal" or "Finn McCool") was a mythical hunter-warrior of Irish mythology, occurring also in the mythologies of Scotland. Mac an Luin means "Son of the Waves" and is also known as "Birga" in some tales. It was said to have a golden hilt.

Fionn was summoned to the Otherworld by Fiachel, who had trained him as a boy. She wanted him to battle with a great serpent, which had been poisoning the Tree of Life with its breath. She gave him an oak shield and blessed his sword, Birga, then sent him down into the earth to kill the wyrm. Fionn fought the serpent for three days and nights before he was able to defeat it. To heal his wounds, Fiachel bathed him and fed him apples, honey and hazelnuts, all foods sacred to the sidhe. Fionn slept in her care before returning home-he had been gone three years, which had seemed like a week in the Otherworld.

Sources:
Fiannaidheacht or Fenian cycle,
    Fianaigecht *translated by Kuno Meyer*

Madman's Stone: A stone located in Dunsang, Ireland. It is believed that if an insane man stands atop of the stone he will recover his reason.

Sources:

'Encyclopaedia of Superstitions, Folklore and the Occult Sciences, Vol. II', by Cora Linn Daniels and C.M. Stevans, J.H. Yewdale and Sons Co. (1903)

Magatama: (勾玉 or 曲玉) are curved beads which first appeared in Japan during the Jōmon period.

They are often found inhumed in mounded tumulus graves as offerings to deities. They continued to be popular with the ruling elites throughout the Kofun Period of Japan, and are often romanticised as indicative of the Yamato Dynasty of Japan. They are mainly made of jade, agate, quartz, talc and jasper. Some consider them to be an Imperial symbol, although in fact ownership was widespread throughout all the chieftainships of Kofun Period Japan. It is believed that magatama were popularly worn as jewels for decoration, in addition to their religious meanings. In this latter regard they were later largely replaced by Buddhist prayer beads in the Nara period.

In modern Japan, the magatama's shape of a sphere with a flowing tail is still the usual visual representation of the human spirit (hitodama). Wearing one during life is considered a way of gaining protection from kami.

Mars, Spear of: A sacred spear of the Roman god Mars was said to be preserved at Rome in the ancient palace of the kings, near the Palatine Hill.

Sources:
(Gellius, N. A. IV. 6; Servius, Virg. Aen. VIII. 3).

<u>Mars, Sword of</u>: The legendary sword of Attila, King of the Huns. Attila believed it to be the sword of the Greek god Mars. According to legend, the sword awarded him victory in all battles he waged.

> *The historian Priscus says it was discovered under the following circumstances: "When a certain shepherd beheld one heifer of his flock limping and could find no cause for this wound, he anxiously followed the trail of blood and at length came to a sword it had unwittingly trampled while nibbling the grass. He dug it up and took it straight to Attila. He rejoiced at this gift and, being ambitious, thought he had been appointed ruler of the whole world, and that through the sword of Mars supremacy in all wars was assured to him.*
> — Jordanes, *The Origin and Deeds of the Goths* ch. XXXV

Although Mars was originally Greek god, it was not uncommon for nomadic warrior tribes to adopt him as their own. The sword of Mars was a vital part of ritual worship of the god; it is known that the Scythians venerated an ancient iron sword called the *achinaches sidareos archaios*, to which they sacrificed animals and prisoners of war (Herodotus, l. IV. 62).

Before Attila, the Huns were scattered in small tribal clusters. Like the Holy Grail that King Arthur sought to bring prosperity to his kingdom, possession of the Sword of Mars meant Attila had the right to control all the Hun tribes and lead them to the western Roman lands.

It may be worthy to note that like modern Christians who "swear to God" that they will do something, it was customary among Romans to pledge vows on the sword of Mars.

Illustration of Attila the Hun, from the Nuremberg Chronicle, by Hartmann Schedel (1440-1514)

Sources:

The History of the Decline and Fall of the Roman Empire. Gibbon, Edward

Prehistoric Dasia. Densusianu, Nicolae (1913) (XXXIX. 2. The reign of Mars)

Masamune swords: Swords forged by the famous 14th century Japanese sword smith master Masamune (also known as Goro Nyudo).

Masamune is considered to be the greatest Japanese sword-smith who ever lived, and many legends have sprouted around the weapons he forged. The swords have a reputation for superior beauty and quality, which is rare for a time when steel was often of poor quality.

When people speak of 'The Masamune', however, they are usually talking about a specific sword Masamune forged for the Tokugawa shogunate family, the "Honjo Masamune" which is considered to be the finest katana ever made. The length of the katana is 65.2 centimeters and the sori is 1.7 centimeters. The sword was made a Japanese National Treasure on May 27th, 1939 C.E. The name "Honjo" possibly came about due to this swords connection with the general Honjo Shigenaga, who gained the sword in battle.

An article in the "Japanese Sword Society of Southern California", relates that in December of 1945 C.E., a descendant of the Tokugawa Shogunate named Tokugawa Iemasa turned possession of the Honjo Masamune and fourteen other swords to the Mejiro Police station in Tokyo. On January 18th 1946 C.E., possession of these swords was turned over to Sergeant Coldy Bimore of the U.S. 7th Cavalry. After this, nothing more is known about the current whereabouts of the Honjo Masamune and it is considered a lost relic.

Signed works of Masamune are rare, so it is often difficult for scholars to verify authentic Masamune blades. However, the "Fudo Masamune", "Kyogoku Masamune", and "Daikoku Masamune" are acceptable as swords that were forged by the legendary swordsmith. There exist many others as well, and they are recorded in Kyôho Meibutsu Cho, a record of excellently forged swords that was written in 1714 C.E. In this record, forty-one swords forged by Masamune are listed.

The few works of Masamune that still exist today all have the Japanese legal status of 'national treasures'.

<u>Mead of Poetry:</u> From Norse mythology, a magical alcoholic beverage that gave the gift of poetry and wisdom to anyone who drank it. It was created by two dwarfs, Fjalar and Galar, who had killed the wisest of the gods, Kvasir, and mixed his blood with honey.

Source:
Encyclopedia of Mythology, Arthur Cotterell

<u>Medham:</u> A sword of the prophet Muhammad, its name means "the keen".

Mercy, Sword of: *See "Curtana"*

Merveilleuse: The sword of Doolin of Mayence, its name means 'wonderful' or 'the marvelous'.

Mímisbrunnr: In Norse Mythology, the magical well of the being Mímir, who was known for his great wisdom. The well was located below the world tree, Yggdrasil, and the waters of the well contained vast wisdom. Mímir drank from the well every morning using the drinking horn Gjallarhorn. (See Gjallarhorn)

The god Odin sought to drink from the well, but Mímir would only allow him to do so if Odin sacrificed one of his eyes in exchange for a drink.

Source:
Encyclopedia of Mythology, Arthur Cotterell

Mimung: A sword from the Anglo-Saxon poem "Waldere", "The Nibelung" and Thidrekssaga Sagas. Mimung was forged by Wieland (Wayland, Weyland, Wetlende or Weland), son of Vadi (Norse), also known as Waetla (German), Wada (Anglo-Saxon), Wate (Middle High German) or Wade (modern English).

Wieland is sometimes mistaken as being Volund, a Norse god, but they are not the same characters. Also Mimung is sometimes mistaken as being Gram, but Gram appears in the Thidrekssaga Saga as the sword of Sigurd—unrelated to Mimung.

Wieland learned smithing from the dwarves of Ballova. Wieland was apparently a genius with metalwork, and forged weapons of incredibly sharpness and durability. Mimung is the most famous of these.

The story goes that Wieland was working as a servant for a king and he accidentally loses the best knife of his patron. Wieland then secretly forges a new knife that is identical, but the king knows something is amiss because the knife cuts far better than ever before. The king questions Wieland but Wieland claims that the king's regular smith Amilias forged it.

The king, having been familiar with Amilias' work, knows Wieland is lieing. Amilias learns of Wieland's actions and challenges the boy to a contest—Amilias will forge a suit of armor and Wieland will forge a sword which will be used to cut the armor that Amilias will be wearing.

Wieland forges a blade in a unique manner; he first forged a regular sword, filed it down to metal shavings, mixed them with flour and fed them to geese. He then collected the bird's excrement, welded the metal shavings together, and forged another sword. He did this process three times until he had a sword that could cut through iron. He named this sword 'Mimung'.

Wieland then forged a second sword nearly identical to Mimung except it was of lesser quality. On the day of the contest, Wieland cuts Amilias and his armor into two pieces so smoothly that it looks as if the sword passed right through him and did no harm. However, Wieland tells the victim to move around and when he does he falls apart.

The king then demands Wieland give him Mimung, and the boy gives the king the lesser quality sword instead, tricking the king into thinking he actually has the fine sword.

Later, Wieland gives possession of the Mimung to Wittich (Witig), his son, who does not want to become a smith, but a hero. Wittich plans to engage King Dietrich of Bern (Thiorek) in battle to earn his renown.

Wittich encounters the heroes Hildebrand, Heime and Hornboge (who unknowningly to Wittich, serve Dietrich—Hildrebrand is actually the mentor to Dietrich), who are on their way to capture a fortress from some robbers. Wittich joins them and uses Mimung to cleave through them, which impresses Hildebrand.

Wittich tells Hildebrand of his intentions to battle Dietrich, and Hildebrand comments Dietrich has become very arraganot and someone should knock him down a few knotches. However, Hildebrand is afraid that Wittich will kill Dietrich, so he decides to secretly switch Wittich's sword with his own in the night.

When Wittich finally reaches Bern, he challenges Dietrich to combat. Dietrich at first refuses, but Hildrebrand convinces his lord to accept the match because Hildebrand is hoping he will be bested in combat.

Dietrich and Wittich do battle, but when Wittich lands a strong blow against the lord, his sword breaks. Dietrich then intends to kill the unarmed boy, but Hildebrand begs his lord to spare the boys life. When Dietrich refuses, Hildebrand returns the sword Mimung to Wittich. The hero defeats Dietrich but spares the king's life out of respect for Hildebrand, and eventually becomes the friend of Dietrich later.

However, Heime becomes jealous of Wittig, and he steals Mimung. When Wittich discovers this, Heime claims he found it so it belongs to him, but he will let Wittich 'borrow' the sword for a battle. However, Wittich becomes angry and attacks Heime, forcing him to admit he had stolen the sword. Wittich regains the sword.

Dietrich once borrowed the sword to defeat Sigfriend (unrelated to, but based on the same Sigfriend that wielded Gram). The Thidrekssaga Saga is full of anarchronisms, placing characters (such as Attila the Hun) in time periods long after they had been dead, or into situations they were not apart of in the older sagas.

Source:
Thidrekssaga Sagas
Nibelungenlied

Mistelteinn: A sword from the Scandanavian Norse Saga of Hrómundr Gripsson. The sword was said to never need sharpening.

Mistelteinn had originally belonged to King Þráinn of Valland, and in his possession killed four-hundred and twenty men, among them the Swedish King Semingr. When Þráinn died, the sword was buried with him. There it remained until Hrómundr accompanied the Danish king Óláfr to loot Þráinn's burial mound. However, Þráinn had become a witch-king (or barrow-wight, sometimes also called a draugr, or "living dead") and no one among the Danish forces would dare enter the tomb to face the undead king except Hrómundr. After a fierce battle, Hrómundr defeated Þráinn and took Mistelteinn for himself.

Hrómundr used the sword to avenge the death of his brothers at the hands of Helgi the Valiant, and to defend King Óláfr in a war against King Haldingr.

Sources:
Hrómundar saga Gripssonar

Mjolnir: The hammer of Thor, the Norse god of thunder. Thor was considered one of the greatest warriors among the gods. The strike of the hammer caused thunderclaps

Mjolnir was a short-handled war hammer meant for throwing.

Image from Nordisk familjebok (a Swedish encylopedia published between 1904–1926) picturing a Thor's hammer.

Sources:
Bulfinch's Mythology. New York: Avenel, 1978.

<u>Moon of the Mountains</u>: A cursed 'moonstone' diamond once owned by Nadir Shah who was murdered by his own troops. The jewel has a particularly bloody history and is believed to bring great misfortune to its bearer, and this has ringed true for many of its owners have been murdered in order for possession of it to be aquired. Two brothers murdered a Jew to get ahold of it, and one brother killed the other to claim the treasure for himself. An Armenian merchant named Shaffrass, by a series of crimes, managed to come into possession of it and it is now set in the imperial scepter of Russia, which just goes to show there may be something to the curse after all.

Sources:
'Encyclopaedia of Superstitions, Folklore and the Occult Sciences, Vol. II', by Cora Linn Daniels and C.M. Stevans, J.H. Yewdale and Sons Co. (1903)

Moralltach
A sword once owned by the Irish god Angus mac Og. Moralltach means "The Great Fury". The sword was said to never miss a stroke.

Angus bequeathed Moralltach to his foster son Diarmuid. When Diarmuid died, his princess Grainne gave the sword to one of their sons.

Morddure
A magical sword that Merlin had made for Arthur in the 'Fairie Queen' by William Spenser.

Mor Glaif
(Also called 'Morglay', Morgelai, 'Glave de la mort') The sword of Sir Bevis of Hampton. The name means 'big bent sword' in Celtic, or 'Big Glaive' in French.

The name seems to have been created by re-arranging the word 'Glaymore' style of sword—which used to be a common spelling of 'Claymore', which is a kind of Scottish two-handed sword.

The sword appears in the English romance 'Bevis of Hampton' (Boeve de Haumlone, an Anglo-Norman story), dating from 1324 C.E.. It also appears in Beuve d'Hanstone and Bovo-Bukh (A Yiddish interpretation written in 1541 C.E. by Elia Levita). Finally, the sword of Bevis and his sword 'Morglay' are recounted in 'Drayton's Hampshire' by Michael Drayton from 1613.

In the tale, Bevis is the son of Count Guy of Hampton. When Bevis is ten (some tales say seven), his mother has Guy assassinated so that she can marry the Emperor of Almaine, Devoun (Doon). When his mother makes plans to kill him too, Bevis' teacher helps him escape to Armenia, and Bevis begins a wild series of adventures

Bevis finds himself in the court Aremnnia's King Ermin, who is taken by the dreadful tale the young boy tells him of his plight. King Ermin asks Bevis to convert to Islam but Bevis refuses, and the king is deeply impressed by the boy's courage to refuse a king. Bevis is then instructed in the ways of a warrior in the hopes he will become a great knight for the King.

When the boy is fifteen, King Brademond demands to marry King Ermin's daughter, Josian, else he destroy Armenia. Bevis (who is in love with the princess, and she with him) asks the king to allow him to lead the army to defeat Brademond and restore peace to the kingdom. King Ermin then knights Bevis and at the wishes of his daughter, bestows him with the sword.

*"The great Armenian King made noble Bevis Knight:
And having raised pow'r, Damascus to invade.
The General of his forces this English hero made.
Then, how fair Josian gave him Arundell his steed,
And Morglay his good sword, in many a gallant deed."*

Bevis then defeats King Brademond in battle and forces him to swear allegiance to King Ermin. When he returns, princess Josian tells Bevis of her love for him and they pledge to marry one another. However, King Brademond is still out for revenge and spreads the rumor that Bevis has taken the princess' virginity; when King Ermin hears this, he orders Bevis to carry a letter to Brademond which is an order for the hero's execution. However, Brademond instead has Bevis imprisoned into a deep pit and fed only bread and water.

Seven years later, Bevis escapes from his captors and discovers Josian has been married off to King Yvor, who also has acquired Mor Glaif. Bevis then sets off to retrieve both his sword and his bride.

By the 16th century, 'morglay' had become a common slang word for 'sword' in England.

In some tales, Mor Glaif had been the sword of Lancelot of the Lake.

Sources:
Dictionary of Phrase and Fable. 1898
Bevis of Hampton

Complete Works of Michael Drayon (Richard Hooper, 1876)

The Romance of Sir Beus of Hamtoun (London:Pub for Early English Text Society by K.Paul, Trench, Trubner & Co, 1885, 1886)

Mouth of Truth: A stone mural in Italy. Popular folklore says that if you put your hand inside it and tell a lie, it will bite off your hand.

Called the *La Bocca della Verità* (in English, "the Mouth of Truth") it is an image, carved from Pavonazzetto marble, of a man-like face, located in the portico of the church of *Santa Maria in Cosmedin* in Rome, Italy. The sculpture is thought to be part of a 1st century ancient Roman fountain, or perhaps a manhole cover, portraying one of several possible pagan gods, probably Oceanus.

The most famous role of the Mouth, however, is its role as a lie detector. Starting from the Middle Ages, it was believed that if one told a lie with one's hand in the mouth of the sculpture, it would be bitten off. The piece was placed in the portico of the Santa Maria in Cosmedin in the 17th century. This church is also home to the supposed relics of Saint Valentine.

Muramasa swords: Swords forged by Muramasa, a famous Japanese swordsmith, known for producing blades of extrodinary sharpness. Legend has it that he was a student of Masamune, but this is impossible since he was born 200 years after Masamune had already died.

Despite this, legends and myths have sprouted up that Muramasa was a failed protégé of Masamune, and created evil, bloodthirsty blades, whereas Masamune created swords that bestowed the wielder with a feeling of internal peace and calm.

A famous story accounts a time where a Masamune and a Muramasa were set down into a stream with the cutting edge facing the current to see whose blade was of superior craftsmanship. Leaf petals were dropped into the stream so that they would speed toward the blades, and while the Muramasa sword cut the leaves perfectly, the Masamune sword cut not a single one—instead, the petals stuck around the blade. This was interpreted to mean that while the Muramasa would not hesitate to kill indiscriminately, the Masamune would not unneedlessly cut that which is innocent and undeserving.

It was also said that while Muramasa was brilliant, he was also insane, and purposely forged blades that would create bloodlust in those who wielded them by test-cutting them on captured criminals.

Another legend says that when Tokugawa Ieyasu became Shogun, he forbid his samurai to ever use a Muramasa because he had lost many friends and relatives to the swords, and once cut himself very badly with one. Given the superstitious nature of the Japanese samurai in regards to swords, this particular legend might be based on fact.

Sources:

Stone, George Cameron (1999). *A Glossary of the Construction, Decoration, and Use of Arms and Armor in All Countries and in All Times.* Dover Publications, Inc., 460. ISBN 0-486-40726-8.

Murasame: Originally a famous fictional rain summoning katana from "Nansō Satomi Hakkenden", a Japanese 19th century novel. It has since appeared in many other forms of media, notably videogames.

Murgleis: Sword of Ganelon, one of the Twelve Peers, who betrays Roland in the Song of Roland.

*"Spurs of fine gold he fastens on his feet,
And to his side Murgleis his sword of steel.
On Tachebrun, his charger, next he leaps."*

The sword is described as having its pommel constructed of gold. Like Durandel, it apparently held relics inside it, but which specific relics are not said.

*"..then answered Guene: 'So be it, as you say.'
On the reics, are in his sword Murgleis,
Treason he's sword, forsworn his faith away."*

Source:
Song of Roland

N

Naegling: A sword that belonged to Beowulf in the epic poem of the same name. Beowulf used this sword to slay a dragon that attacked his kingdom. Naegling was Beowulf's family sword, but it shattered in line 2681 of the epic poem.

Nagastra: A celestial weapon invoked by Karna, one of the important characters of the *'Mahābhārata'*, from Hindu mythology.

Before the Kurukshetra War where Karna was fated to battle Arjuna, son of the God King Idra, to the death, Karna promises his mother he will not use a divine weapon more than once. During the battle Karna invoked Nagastra against Arjuna in battle, but missed, and thus was unable to attack Arjuna again. Karna was thus defeated by Arjuna.

Sources:
'Mahābhārata'

Nagelring: (Naglhring) A sword used by of King Dietrich of Bern, and later Heime. It means 'nail-ring'. It was said to be very beautiful and magnificent. It appears in the Thidrekssaga Saga.

The story goes that Dietrich saves the life of a dwarf named Alfrek, who tells the hero the location of a wonderful treasure and a powerful sword, but to get it he must promise to defeat defeat the giants Grim and Hild, a married couple.

Alfrek gives Dietrich Nagelring (which he had stolen from the giants) when the hero agrees to do so.

Dietrich later, when he gets the Eckisax sword, gives Nagelring to Heime, son of Strudder, who was one of his vassals.

Dietrich was loosely based on the historical King Theodoric the Great (454-526 AD) who ruled Italy, but greatly exaggerated, and since the Thidrekssaga Saga Saga was written in 1205 in Germany, it cannot be considered 'true Norse mythology'—but it was certainly based on it.

Nehushtan: (Hebrew "NChShThN", or "thing of brass") In the Old Testament of the Christian Bible, Numbers 21:9-9, this is the serpent of brass made by Moses and set up on a pole to cure the Israelites of venmous bites caused by fiery serpents in the wilderness.

Nihongo: One of the Three Great Spears of Japan. Also romanized as Nippongo.
The spear was once used in the Imperial Palace (?) and then became the weapon of Masanori Fukushima, and then Tahei Mori gained possession of it. It is currently kept at the Fukuoka City Musuem.

Ninon de L'Enclos, Skull of: The skull of Ninon de L'Enclos (also spelled as Ninon de Lenclos). She lived through November 10th, 1620 to October 17th, 1705. She was a French author, courtesan and patron of the arts. Born Anne de Lenclos, Ninon was a nickname her father gave her.

Folklore says that in the 18th century, Maria Leszczynska, then queen of France, would kneel before the skull and say her prayers to it.

For the time period, the practice was not uncommon in the region. Called "the pretty darling", a skull illuminated with tapers and highly decorated was considered the proper furnishings of a devout lady's boidoir.

The practice may have stemmed from the orthodox Greek tradition of saying prayers to icons, or drawings of saints, in the hopes that the saints would stand before God and personally intercede on their behalf.

Sources:
 'Encyclopaedia of Superstitions, Folklore and the Occult Sciences, Vol. II', by Cora Linn Daniels and C.M. Stevans, J.H. Yewdale and Sons Co. (1903)

O

Odyssus, Bow of: A mythological Greek artifact that is associated with Odysseus' power and his reign as king.

Odysseus is a Greek king of legendary proportions. He was the king of Ithaca and revered in Homer's poem Odyssey and also played an enigmatic role in Homers' Iliad. Odysseus was the husband of Penelope and they had a son named Telemachus. Odysseus was the child of Laertes and Anticlea.

Odysseus was known and revered for his luminosity, craftiness and adaptability and was thus known widely as Odysseus the Cunning for his smart and slyness mixed with his intelligence made him a brilliant ruler. Odysseus is most famously known for the ten exciting years he took on the journey home after the Trojan war.

Odysseus bow is famous for being able to shoot an arrow through tweleve axe shafts but he didn't take it to the Trojan war. It is said that in the competition for who could string the bow of Apollo and all the suitors present tried to string Apollo's bow but failed miserably. Odysseus is said to have come forward in disguise and not only strings the bow but shoots the arrow and wins the competition.

The bow of Odysseus is significant for its immense power and yielding strength. Being the bow of Apollo which was impossible to string and even more difficult to shoot an arrow from, Odysseus has so far been deemed the only person in Greek mythology to not only string the bow but to throw arrows from it.

The bow is not described with any physical attributes except us knowing of its great power. It is known to be very light in weight and small that everyone even a woman such as Penelope could pick it up but its string is deemed to be tough and unstring able.

Apparently Odysseus got his bow made from someone in Lacedaemon. The man he bought it from was called Iphitus. Odysseus gave a sword and spear to Iphitus in exchange for the bow. In the Trojan war however Odysseus does not carry the bow for war but left it in a treasure chamber of his house on a peg. The bow is accompanied by a quiver full of bronze heavy weight arrows.

Odysseus' bow served great purpose in helping him achieve his goals of conquest of surrounding empires and in his effort to keep his family together. However Odysseus had another son, not from Penelope and was forced to come face to face with him.

Odysseus' bow is a representation of his great power, cunning and sharp mind and his ability to fight for what he believed in. His bow though light weight and airy could only be used by him and strung by him.

Ogma, Whip of: The spear of Ogma (the Celtic sun god) is used to "guide the passage of the invisible sun

Oil of Magic: In Gnostic tradition, an item received by Adam from his son Seth. The oil came from the Tree of Mercy.

Sources:
'Encyclopaedia of Superstitions, Folklore and the Occult Sciences, Vol. II', by Cora Linn Daniels and C.M. Stevans, J.H. Yewdale and Sons Co. (1903)

Olsa-Big Knife, Sword of: In the Arthurian legends which surround the 'Quest of the Holy Grail' one of the tasks which any Knight wishing to find the Holy Grail needed to overcome was the crossing of the 'sword-bridge'. This was accomplished by locating the 'Sword of Olsa-Big Knife' and placing it over the gap between a cliff and the 'Grail Castle' where the holy chalice resided.

In related tales, Olsa-Big Knife was an ally of Arthur, and in the story of 'Culhwch and Olwen' his sword was used by Arthur to cross a river.

Orihalcum: A legendary metal mentioned in several ancient writings, most notably the story of Atlantis as recounted in the *Critias* dialogue, recorded by Plato. It is sometimes spelled as *aurichalcum*.

According to Critias, orichalcum was considered second only to gold in value, and was found and mined in many parts of Atlantis in ancient times. By the time of Critias, however, it was known only by name.

The name derives from the original Greek, meaning literally "mountain copper" or "copper mountain". The Romans transliterated "orichalcum" as "aurichalcum," which was thought to mean "gold copper". It is known from the writings of Cicero that the metal they called orichalcum, while it resembled gold in colour, had a much lower value.

In 2015, a number of ingots believed to be orichalcum were discovered in a sunken vessel (in the coasts of Gela in Sicily), which has tentatively been dated as being 2600 years old. Analyzed with X-ray fluorescence by Dario Panetta, of TQ - Tecnologies for Quality, the 39 ingots turned out to be an alloy consisting of 75-80 percent copper, 15-20 percent zinc, and smaller percentages of nickel, lead and iron.

Sources:
"Unusual Metal Recovered from Ancient Greek Shipwreck - Archaeology Magazine" Jessica E. Saraceni

<u>Orna</u>: A mythological sword from Iris mythology. Once owned by Tethra, King of the Fomor, who was killed in battle. Orna had the power to tell of all the deeds that had been done by it.

Ogma, the 'Warrior of the Tautha de Danaan', reclaimed the sword at the second battle of Magh Tuireadh.

"It was in this battle Ogma found Orna, the sword of Tethra, a king of the Fomor, and he took it from its sheath and cleaned it. And when the sword was taken out of the sheath, it told all the deeds that had been done by it, for there used to be that power in swords."

Sources:
Book of Invasions

<u>Olyndicus, Spear of:</u> The lance of Olyndicus, the celtiberians' war chief who fought against Rome. According to Florus, he wielded a silver lance that was sent to him by the gods from the sky.

<u>Otegine:</u> One of the Three Great Spears of Japan.

<u>Ǒusībùyúnlǚ:</u> (藕絲步雲履)/"cloud-stepping boots" or "cloud-stepping shoes", used by Sun Wukong in Journey to the West. They allow him to ride on clouds.

Made of lotus fiber, these are one of the treasures of the Dragon Kings; Ào Ming gives them to Monkey in order to get rid of him when he acquires the Rúyì Jīn Gū Bàng.

P

Palladium: A statue of the Goddess Minerva that fell from the sky and was revered by the citizens of Troy.

The Palladium is described in legend as a wooden statue of Athena, although some tales imply it was her childhood companion Pallas. Electra, the daughter of Atlas, clung to the statue in the hope it would prevent Zeus from raping her. Zeus threw the Palladium out of Olympus. The statue was found in the tent of Ilus, the founder of the city of Ilium or Troy. The Palladium was said to protect Troy from invaders, however Heracles and Telamon had captured the city in Lacemedon's reign.

According to legend, when the image of the goddess was discovered, Ilus, the founder of Troy, thought it was a good omen. The Trojans believed that as long as it remained within their gates, their city would be unconquerable.

It protected Troy, during the great Trojan War, until in the final stage of the war, Odysseus and Diomedes stole the Palladium from the temple of Athena, at the advice of the captured Trojan seer, Helenus, the son of Priam and Hecuba. However, according to Vergil, the Palladium that the Greeks had stolen was a fake. Aeneas the only surviving leader of the war, took the Palladium with him when he settled in Italy. The Palladium was said to have been in the temple of Vesta in Rome.

Sources:
'*Encyclopaedia of Superstitions, Folklore and the Occult Sciences, Vol. II*', by Cora Linn Daniels and C.M. Stevans, J.H. Yewdale and Sons Co. (1903)

<u>Pandora's Box</u>: In Greek mythology, Pandora's box is the large jar (πιθος *pithos*) carried by Pandora (Πανδώρα) that contained evils to be unleashed on mankind — ills, toils and sickness — and finally hope.

After Prometheus' theft of the secret of fire, Zeus ordered Hephaestus to create the woman Pandora as part of the punishment for mankind. Pandora was given many seductive gifts from Aphrodite, Hermes, Hera, Charites, and Horae (according to *Works and Days*).

For fear of additional reprisals, Prometheus warned his brother Epimetheus not to accept any gifts from Zeus, but Epimetheus did not listen, and married Pandora. Pandora had been given a large jar and instruction by Zeus to keep it closed, but she had also been given the gift of curiosity, and ultimately opened it. When she opened it, all of the evils, ills, diseases, and burdensome labor that mankind had not known previously, escaped from the jar, but it is said, that at the very bottom of her box, there lay hope.

The original Greek word used for the box was 'pithos', which is a large jar, sometimes as large as a small person. It was used for storage of wine, oil, grain or other provisions, or, ritually, as a container for a human body for burying. In the case of Pandora this jar may have been made of clay for use as storage as in the usual sense, or of metal, such as bronze, as an unbreakable prison

Pashupata: The ultimate weapon of Shiva, which could be thrown from his mind, eyes, words or shot as an arrow. It can destroy all of creation instantly.

Peleus, Sword of: A magic sword that makes its wielder victorious in the battle or the hunt, used by the Greek hero Peleus.

Pernik Sword: A medieval sword found near the village of Pernik, Bulgaria, in 1921.

The sword bore a strange inscription written in silver,

+IHININIHVILPIDHINIHVILPN+

In 2005 C.E., the inscription was discovered to be written in an early West Germanic language meaning "I do not await eternity; I am eternity."

The weapon is mentioned here not because of its attachment to a particular myth or legend, but because it is a sheer historical oddity.

Perseus, Sword of: A sword given to Perseus by the Greek goddess Athena. Depending on the telling, the sword was made of either diamonds or 'adamant', and forged by the god Hephaistos.

Athena gave the sword along with a highly polished shield to Perseus to help him slay Medusa.

"He [Perseus] is said to have received from Volcanus [Hephaistos] a knife made out of adamant, with which he killed Medusa the Gorgon." - Hyginus, Astronomica 2.12

"Perseus" by Benvenuto Cellini, Loggia dei Lanzi, Florence, Italy

Source:
Hyginus, Astronomica 2.12

<u>Philippan</u>: The sword of Antony in William Shakespeare's famous play *'Antony and Cleopatra'*. It was named because it was used in the battle of Philippi. The sword was given to Antony by Cleopatra but it was lost when the Emperor Augustus (Octavian) defeats him at Actium.

<u>Polycrates, Ring of</u>: A ring that belonged to Polycrates, the King of Samos. In the year 230 of the

building of Rome (?), the king, deciding to test his level of good fortune, threw one of his most valuable rings into the sea in order to test whether it would somehow return to him. The next day during his dinner meal, the ring was found in the belly of a fish that had been served to him. The ring was regarded as a good luck talisman and given a place among the royal treasures in the Temple of Concord.

This ring is also the subject of a ballad by Schiller.

Sources:
'Encyclopaedia of Superstitions, Folklore and the Occult Sciences, Vol. II', by Cora Linn Daniels and C.M. Stevans, J.H. Yewdale and Sons Co. (1903)

Poseidon, Trident of: The trident of Poseidon, used to create water sources in Greece, and horses. Greek mythology.

Precieuse: Sword of Baligant, admiral of Babylonia who comes to Marsile's aid in the Song of Roland tale.

Baligant names the sword Precieuse, meaning 'precise', after he hears that Charlemagne's magic sword is named 'Joyeuse'. The sword's name was used as a Saracen battle cry.

Source:
Chanson de Roland

Q

<u>Qual'i</u>: Also known as 'Qul'ay', this is one of the nine relic swords of the Prophet Muhammad of Islamic legend. It is said that the grandfather of Muhammad found this sword when he uncovered the 'Well of Zamzam' in Mecca.

The blade is 100 cm in length, and engraved in Arabic with the words "This is the noble sword of the house of Muhammad the prophet, the apostle of God". The blade is unique from the other nine swords in that it has a wave-light design on it.

<u>Quern-biter</u>: The sword of Haco I of Norway, (Hacon the Good) its name means 'foot-breadth'. The sword was also used by Thoralf Skolinsons (Thoral the Strong) of Norway.

"Quen-biter of Hakon the Good,
Wherewith at a stroke he hewed,
The millstone through and through
And Foot-breadth of Thoralf the Strong,
Were neither so broad nor so long,
Nor so true as Olaf's sword."

Source:
King Olaf's Christimas

R

Refil: The sword of Regin the dwarf in the Norse Nibelungen saga. It might have been based on Ridill.

According to the *Skáldskaparmál*, Refil is also the name of the sword of Regin, brother of Fafnir.

Rhongomiant: The spear of King Arthur. Arthur used the spear to defeat Sir Thomas of Wolford during a duel.

Source:
Matter of Britain

Ridill: The sword Sigurd (Sigfriend) uses to cut the heart of Fafnir the dragon before he eats it, thus gaining Fafnir's powers. The sword was one of the treasures of Fafnir that Sigurd claimed.

Romulus' Rod: A crooked rod that belonged to Romulus, the founder of Rome. In the Roman tradition, soothsayers used the rod to describe the quarters of heaven when they sat to observe the flight of birds for good or bad fortune. The rod was kept in the palatium until it was lost when Rome fell under siege by the Gauls, but when the city was taken back the rod was re-discovered under burning ruins and heaps of ashes, miraculously untouched by the fire.

Sources:

'Encyclopaedia of Superstitions, Folklore and the Occult Sciences, Vol. II', by Cora Linn Daniels and C.M. Stevans, J.H. Yewdale and Sons Co. (1903)

<u>Rotti</u>: (Also spelled Hrotti) One of the swords Sigurd claims as bounty when he takes the treasure of Fafnir after he kills the dragon.

<u>Round Table</u>: From the Arthurian myths. Merlin created the Round Table as a wedding present for Arthur and Guinevere. It was magical in nature and could fold up into a pocket.

In other tales, the Round Table was actually commissioned by Uther Pendragon, Arthur's father, and Merlin created it based on Uther's desire to have a table where 150 knights could see each other and sit without quarrelling about sitting order.

The Round Table served many purposes; it prevented arguments over precendence, it was a symbol of wholeness and honored the table of the last supper of Jesus Christ.

S

Sakhrat: According to Mohammedan mythology, a sacred stone that rests on Mount Kaf, the home of giants and fairies. Anyone who possesses a single grain of the stone has the power to work miracles. The stone is described as being the color of an emerald, and its reflection gives off the blint tint of the sky.

Sources:
 'Encyclopaedia of Superstitions, Folklore and the Occult Sciences, Vol. II', by Cora Linn Daniels and C.M. Stevans, J.H. Yewdale and Sons Co. (1903)

Sanchu: (Also called Sancho) The sword of Eck.

Sanglamore: The sword of Braggadochio in the Faerie Queene. It means "Big Bloody Glaive".

Sansamha: The sword of Haroun-al-Rascid from The Book of One Thousand and One Nights.

Satan's Trident: In Christian mythology, this is the trident often wielded by the king of devils, Satan. It may be related to poisiod's trident. It also served as his scepter.

Traditional image of devils poking people in the butt with tridents comes from this imagery.

Sauvagine: A sword of Ogier the Dane from the 'Song of Roland'. It was a sword forged by Munifican. Its name means 'relentless' and it took three years to forge like all the other swords in the poem.

Scone, Stone of: Also commonly known as the Stone of Destiny or the Coronation Stone (though the former name sometimes refers to Lia Fáil) is a block of sandstone historically kept at the now-ruined abbey in Scone, near Perth, Scotland. It was used for centuries in the coronation of the monarchs of Scotland, the monarchs of England, and, more recently, British monarchs. Other names by which it has sometimes been known include Jacob's Pillow Stone and the Tanist Stone.

Traditionally the Stone of Scone (pronounced as 'skoon') is said to have originally been the pillow stone used by the Biblical Jacob, referring to an episode in the Book of Genesis (28:10-18) when the Hebrew patriarch Jacob was running from home after getting the blessing of the first born from his father Isaac, he came to a place where he rested his head on a stone and then consecrated it after God appeared to him in a dream.

According to another legend, the Stone of Scone was originally the Coronation Stone of the early Dál Riata Gaels when they lived in Ireland, which they brought with them when settling Caledonia. Another legend holds that the stone was actually the travelling altar used by Saint. Columba in his missionary activities throughout what is now Scotland. Certainly, since the time of Kenneth Mac

Alpin, the first King of Scots, at around 847, Scottish monarchs were seated upon the stone during their coronation ceremony. At this time the stone was situated at Scone, a few miles north of Perth.

<u>Schamir:</u> Also known as the Stone of Wisdom, this was a mystical object owned by King Solomon. The only way to get one like it was to cover up the nest of the moor-hen so that it could not get to its young. The nest was to be covered with a piece of glass or crystal, so that, seeing its babies, the hen would go and get this magic stone with which to drop upon the glass to break it. At that moment, the hen must be frightened away so that the stone could be retrieved.

When King Solomon played this trick on a moor-hen to get his stone, the stone he received was one that belonged to the Prince of the Sea. The hen was so dismayed by her disloyalty to the god that she slew herself.

Sources:
 '*Encyclopaedia of Superstitions, Folklore and the Occult Sciences, Vol. II*', by Cora Linn Daniels and C.M. Stevans, J.H. Yewdale and Sons Co. (1903)

<u>Schrit</u>: (Also spelled Schritt) The sword of Biterolf (Biterulf), King of Toledo, from the Norwegian Thidrekssaga written in 1205. Schrit means 'The Lopper'.

The sword was used by Biterolf and his son Dietleib (Thetleif) to defeat Gunther, Hagen and Sigfried in combat with the help of Dietrich—although this story is entirely unrelated to the ancient Norse myths and legends.

Seal of Solomon: In various Judeo-Christian and Islamic medieval legends, a magical signet ring worn by King Solomon that gave him the power to command demons (jinni) and speak with animals.

In an Arabian Nights story, an evil djinn is imprisioned inside a copper bottle for 1,800 years by a lead seal stamped by the ring. Other books such as the Psuedomonarchi Daemonum describe many more demons being imprisioned inside the bottle in a similar fashion.

In some versions the ring was made of brass and iron, carved with the Name of God and set with four jewels. Later versions described the signet as a hexagram like the Star of David, and in yet other stories the seal is what we would recognize today as a pentagram.

Seven-Branched Sword: The Seven-Branched Sword (also called "Nanatsusaya no tachi" in Japanese and "Chiljido" in Korean)

The Seven-Branched Sword is one of the national treasures of Japan and numerous replicas are displayed in museums throughout Korea. It is also known as the Seven-Branched Knife or Seven-Pronged Spear or Seven-Pronged Sword. It was probably made in Korea but some sources advocate a Chinese origin.

The sword is made of iron and has six branch-like protrusions on the sides with the tip of the sword counting as the seventh branch. The seven branches of the sword suggests a tree-motif connected with the Shamanistic traditions of Korea. It is 74.9 centimeters in length. The sword is a highlight of the metal-working skills of the Baekje. The sword is currently housed in the Isonokami Shrine in Japan and has an inscribed date of Taiwa 4 which corresponds to year 369 CE. The date on the sword is close enough that it corroborates with a story in the Nihon Shoki of a sword sent by the Baekje King Geunchogo in 372 CE by the Korean envoy Kutei to the Empress Regent Jingu. However, one must add a requisite 120 years (two sexagenary cycles) to the dates mentioned in the Nihon Shoki to corroborate the date of the story with the true date of the sword's manufacture.

There is a two-sided inscription on the sword which is inlaid in gold. The inscription is the cause of much controversy between Korean and Japanese historians. The inscription states (brackets showing unreadable words):

In English:
First Side: "This seven-branched sword was made of [], refined many times, at noon on the eleventh (?) day of the [] month, fourth year of Taihe (?) era. [] repels the enemy and is fit for a king or a duke (?). Made by []."

Second Side: "Never before has there been such a blade. The [] of Baekje [], who owes his life to august Jin, had this sword made for King 'Shi' of Wa in the hope that it might be passed on to later generations."

Most historians agree that the sword was made, or commissioned by, most likely the king of Baekje, or at least a high-ranking member of the court, as a gift to the Wa ruler 'Shi.'

<u>Seven League Boots:</u> Magical boots which allow the person wearing them to take strides of seven leagues per step, resulting in great speed. The boots are often presented by a magical character to the protagonist to aid in the completion of a significant task. These boots appear in a number of stories but most notably Hop-o'-My-Thumb (le petit Poucet) where the protagonist steals the boots from an ogre.

<u>Seven Star Sword</u>: In the Chinese folktale 'Bei You Ji' (Pei-yu-chi), the hero of the tale, Xuantian Shangdi, is given this sword by the Jade Emperor to subdue the powers of evil. The sword allows the hero to channel 'true water' to vanquish fire demons.

Source:
Journey to the North: An Ethnohistorical Analysis and Annotated Translation of the Chinese Folk Novel *Pei-yu-Chi* Berkeley University of California Press (1987)

<u>Shamshir-e Zomorrodnegar</u>: The supposed sword of King Solomon from the Persian epic Amir Arsalan. Its name means, "Emerald studded sword".

In the tale a witch creates a horned demon called Fulad-zereh who is invincible against all weapons except the Shamsir-e Zomorrodnegar.

The sword was also a powerful charm against magic, and any wound inflicted by the sword could only be treated by a special potion made from many rare ingredients, one of which was Fulad-zereh's brains.

The hero of the story, Arsalan, gains possession of the sword and uses it to slay both the demon and the witch.

Source:
Amir Arsalan

Shichishitō: A sword passed down as a divine treasure (*shinpō*) in the treasury of Isonokami Jingū. Originally housed in the shrine and treated as an object of worship, the sword was displayed in the shrine's Divine Procession (*shinkōsai*) called the "Divine Procession of Swords" held annually on the thirtieth day of the sixth month. The sword functioned as a temporary dwelling or "spirit vessel" (*mitamashiro*) for the *kami* during the ritual.

With a length of 74.9 cm, the *shichishitō* is a special kind of sword in which each side of the body bears three branching blades. Because of rust, it is difficult to discern any longer the raised ridge running along the middle of the main blade, but it is apparent that the blade has a gold inlay of thirty-four characters on the front and twenty-seven on the back. A paraphrase of the inscription states that "on the sixteenth day of the fourth (or fifth) month of the fourth year of the Taiwa era (1204-5), one hundred shichishitō were made, and military defeat was avoided as a result." The inscription continues, stating that "such swords are suitable for gifts to one's lord. There is no evidence of these swords before this time. The King of Paekche and the Prince are bound by mutual favor and thus the *shichishitō* have been made at the request of the King of Yamato. May they be handed down to future generations eternally." It is believed that the entry in the *Nihongi* for the ninth month of the fifty-second year of the reign of Empress Jingū; refers to this sword, as it records a messenger from the King of Paekche presenting the court with a shichishitō and a *nanatsuko* mirror. The *shichishitō* has thus been designated a National Treasure due to its importance for our knowledge of foreign relations in ancient times.

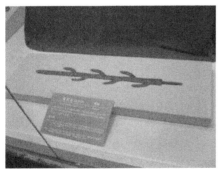

This replica of the Chiljido is held at the War Memorial in Seoul, South Korea.

Sources:

Hall, John Whitney (1993). Delmer M. Brown: *The Cambridge History of Japan Vol. 1*. Cambridge University Press, p. 123. ISBN 0-521-22352-0.

Wagner, Donald B. (1993). *Iron and steel in Ancient China*. Brill Academic Publishers, p. 283. ISBN 90-04-09632-9.

Covell, Jon C.; Covell, Alan C. (1984). *Korean Impact on Japanese Culture*. Hollym International Corp., p. 22. ISBN 0-930878-34-5.

Hong, Wontack [1994]. "Chapter 5: Background Materials, 4. The Seven-Branched Sword", *Peakche of Korea and the Origin of Yamato Japan* (PDF), Seoul: Kudara International, pp. 251-254. ISBN 89-85567-02-0.

Sakamoto, Tarō (1991). *The Six National Histories of Japan*, trans. John S. Brownlee, UBC Press, pp. 62-63. ISBN 0-7748-0379-7.

Farris, William Wayne (1998). *Sacred Texts and Buried Treasures*. University of Hawaii Press, pp. 64-66. ISBN 0-8248-2030-4.

Farris, William Wayne (1998). *Sacred Texts and Buried Treasures*. University of Hawaii Press, p. 114. ISBN 0-8248-2030-4.

Shylock, Ring of: A magical ring made of turquoise that was owned by Shylock, a character in William Shakespeare's *The Merchant of Venice*. Shylock's deceased wife, Leah gave it to him when he was a bachelor in order to win his heart and encourage him to propose to her. The ring was magical, possessing vast talismanic properties, but failed to forewarn him of the loss of his daughter and his wealth.

Sources:
'Encyclopaedia of Superstitions, Folklore and the Occult Sciences, Vol. II', by Cora Linn Daniels and C.M. Stevans, J.H. Yewdale and Sons Co. (1903)

<u>Sif, Golden Tresses of:</u> In Norse mythology Loki tricked the beautiful Sif into shaving her head. The Golden Tresses of Sif are the wig made to replace her hair. The Golden Tresses moulded themselves to Sif's head and even grew longer like real hair.

In Skáldskaparmál, Snorri relates a story where Loki cuts off Sif's hair as a prank. When Thor discovers this, he grabs hold of Loki, resulting in Loki swearing to have a headpiece made of gold to replace Sif's locks. Loki fulfills this promise by having a headpiece made by dwarfs, the Sons of Ivaldi. Along with the headpiece, the dwarfs produced Odin's spear, Gungnir. As the story progresses, the incident leads to the creation of the ship Skíðblaðnir and the boar Gullinbursti for Freyr, the multiplying ring Draupnir for Odin, and the mighty hammer Mjöllnir for Thor.

Source:
Prose Edda

<u>Silver Bullet:</u> The idea of the werewolf's supposed vulnerability to silver probably dates back to the legend of the Beast of Gévaudan, in which a gigantic

wolf is killed by a person wielding a gun loaded with silver bullets.

In the Brothers Grimm fairy-tale of *The Two Brothers*, a bullet-proof witch is shot down by silver buttons, fired from a gun.

Singing Sword of Coronary Mor:
The sword of the High King Coronary Mor (Conarire Mor, Conary Mor), of Irish mythology. Like its name suggests, it was capable of singing songs.

Skíðblaðnir:
A magical boat that appears in Norse mythology. It was owned by Freyr, though often used by Odin. It could hold all the Æsir and their horses yet it could fold so you could fit it in your pocket. Once the sails were lifted a steady breeze would always come.

It is attested in the *Poetic Edda*, compiled in the 13th century from earlier traditional sources, and in the *Prose Edda* and *Heimskringla*, both written in the 13th century by **Snorri Sturluson**.

Skofnung:
Magical sword used by Kormak Ogmundsson the Skald so that he could battle his enemy Bersi, who wielded the magic sword Whitting.

The sword had originally belonged to Hrólfr Kraki, (*Hroðulf, Rolfo, Roluo, Rolf Krage*) a legendary Danish king. Skofnung was imbued with the souls of the king's twelve berserkers bodyguards, thus endowed with supernatural durability and sharpness.

In the Laxdœla Saga, it is explained that Hrólfr was buried with the sword, but his grave was plundered by Midfjardar-Skeggi, who passed the sword down to his son Eid of Ás, who in turn gave it to Thorkel Eyjólfsson. Thorkel's son Gellir becomes the last person to wield Skofnung in the saga.

Kormak borrowed Skofnung from Skeggi of Midfjord, but he gave the warrior specific instructions on how to withdraw the sword from its scabbard:

"Hard will you find it to handle,' said Skeggi. 'There is a pouch to it, and that you shall let be. Sun must not shine on the pommel of the hilt. You shall not wear it until fighting is forward, and when you come to the field, sit all alone and then draw it. Hold the edge toward you, and blow on it. Then will a little worm creep from under the hilt. Then slope the sword over, and make it easy for that worm to creep back beneath the hilt."

However, Kormack ignored these instructions and tried to force the sword out of its scabbard, which upset the sword. When Kormack engages Bersi in battle, Skofnung slices off the tip of Whitting's blade, but the shard stabs Kormack's hand—he ends up losing the match because of it.

According to Eid of Ás in chapter 57 of the Laxdœla saga, the sword is not to be drawn in the presence of women, and that the sun must never shine on the sword's hilt. It is also told by Eid that any wound made by Skofnung will not heal unless rubbed with the Skofnung Stone, which Eid gives to Thorkel Eyjólfsson along with the sword.

Sources:
Kormack's Saga Ogmundsson
Hrólfr Kraki's saga
Laxdœla Saga

Staff of Sun Wukong: An iron rod that changes size according to the whim of the user, it was originally used by Da Yu to measure the depth of the flood waters destroying ancient China.

It was later stolen by Sun Wukong the Monkey King from the Eastern Sea Dragon King, Ao Guang, it can shrink into size of a hair, but when extended it was massive and heavy. Called "Ruyi Jingu Bang" (Pinyin) meaning "As you will Golden Bound Cudgel".

Sun Wukong usually kept it the size of a sewing needle behind his ear when not in battle.

Source:
"Journey to the West".

Staff of Moses: According to the Book of Exodus in the Bible, the staff used by Moses (Hebrew: matteh, translated "rod" in the King James Bible).

The staff was used to perform a variety of miracles such as causing water to appear from a rock, was transformed into a snake, and was also used to part the Red Sea.

State, Sword of: A ceremonial sword that is part of the British Royal Crown Jewels kept at the Tower of London.

There are five swords now kept in the Tower. The largest of these is the Sword of State, with a blade about thirty-two inches long. The grip and the pommel are of gilt metal, and the former bears designs of the portcullis, fleur-de-lys, and harp, whilst on the latter are a thistle, orb, and other emblems. The scabbard itself is covered with crimson velvet encircled with gilded metal plates bearing designs in high relief.

The Jewelled Sword of State is considered to be the most beautiful and valuable sword in the world. It was made for George IV., at a cost of £6000, and presents a mass of jewels of all colours set in gold.

At the Coronation this sword is borne by the Keeper of the Jewel House as one of the military emblems, and is offered by the King in homage to the Church.

The Spurs are of solid gold, richly chased in flowing patterns, and have straps of crimson velvet embroidered in gold. They are known as St. George's Spurs, and are one of the emblems of knighthood and chivalry, and with the sword help to mark the military character of the Sovereign.

At the Coronation these spurs are presented to the Sovereign, and immediately deposited on the Altar, being afterwards redeemed by the payment of some handsome fee.

The Sword of State

Stone of Death: Located in Nasu, Japan.

Sources:
 '*Encyclopaedia of Superstitions, Folklore and the Occult Sciences, Vol. II*', by Cora Linn Daniels and C.M. Stevans, J.H. Yewdale and Sons Co. (1903)

Stone, Philosopher's: A legendary result of alchemy, a metallurgical science that predated modern chemistry. Alchemy was practiced throughout the world, including the Middle East, Europe and Asia; and studied until the dawn of science. The Rosicucians and even famous individuals such as Issac Newton considered it a serious subject of study.

The Philosopher's Stone was a required component for the transmutation of lesser metals into gold, however many alchemix texts warn that "our gold is not of the common kind"; Alchemic texts were often written in riddle form to conceil their true meaning to the uninitiated.

The Philosopher's Stone could also be used to create a variety of other magical properties; alkahest, an imaginary liquid reputed to be a universal menstruum capable of resolving all bodies into their constituent elements; the panacea, a remedy to cure all diseases; and the elixir vitae, a cordial which could sustain life indefinetly.

The first Philosopher's Stone was, according to legend, owned by Noah, used to light and warm the ark for all the living creatures aboard his ship during the biblical flood.

Whether a Philosopher's Stone was ever created or not, what is certain is that the pursuit of its creation brought about many technological advances such as the invention of gunpowder by Berthold Schwartz; the Dresden porcelain manufacture by Botticher; and the properties of acids by Geber.

Some texts describe the stone was being a red powder of amalgam; it should be pointed out, however, that the word "stone" in alchemy does not mean the mineral variety, but the substratum of article employed to produce a certain effect.

Sources:
'Encyclopaedia of Superstitions, Folklore and the Occult Sciences, Vol. II', by Cora Linn Daniels and C.M. Stevans, J.H. Yewdale and Sons Co. (1903)

Stone of St. Patrick: Also known as St. Patrick's Stone. Located on the isle of Shannon, it is believed that if anyone drinks from the water that fills in the hollow of the top, that person will be cured of any disease.

Sources:
'Encyclopaedia of Superstitions, Folklore and the Occult Sciences, Vol. II', by Cora Linn Daniels and C.M. Stevans, J.H. Yewdale and Sons Co. (1903)

Stone of Tongues: A stone given to the King of Lombardy by his father the dwarf Elberich. When put into the mouth the stone endowed the person to perfectly speak any foreign language.

Sources:
'Encyclopaedia of Superstitions, Folklore and the Occult Sciences, Vol. II', by Cora Linn Daniels and C.M. Stevans, J.H. Yewdale and Sons Co. (1903)

Stone, Wealth-Giving: Located in Eoshima, Japan. Pilgrims pray to it.

Sources:
'Encyclopaedia of Superstitions, Folklore and the Occult Sciences, Vol. II', by Cora Linn Daniels and C.M. Stevans, J.H. Yewdale and Sons Co. (1903)

Stone, Women's: Located at the temple of Hachiman in Kamakura, Japan.

Sources:
'Encyclopaedia of Superstitions, Folklore and the Occult Sciences, Vol. II', by Cora Linn Daniels and C.M. Stevans, J.H. Yewdale and Sons Co. (1903)

Szczerbiec: Sword of Polish kings, used in Coronation ceremonies. The weapon is sometimes called 'The Jagged Sword', or 'notched sword'. A (very) rough pronunciation of the sword's name in english is 'sh-ch-eh-rr-bee-ets'.

Various legends link the sword with the first king of Poland, Boleslaus the Brave (992-1025). The sword gained the title 'Jagged Sword' when Boleslaus damaged the blade against the Golden Gate in Kiev when he victiously entered the captured city in 1018.

The sword is 98 centimeters long, and the golden hilt bears many unique esoteric symbols and inscriptions. First of all, the design of the guard is of a 'Templar sword', and the pommel has a large sigil depicting the letter 'T' with the Greek letters 'Alpha' and 'Omega' surrounded by a cross. Given this symbology, the 'T' is thought to stand for 'Templum', or the 'Order of the Knights Templar', who possess the Alpha and Omega of all knowledge.

An inscription runs around the pommel that reads 'This figure serves to love kings and princes who judge contentions'. Another pair of inscriptions appear on both sides of the guard:

"Whoever carries these names of God I with him will never suffer any danger." ('God I' is interpreted to imply the first letter of the Tetragrammaton, the holy name of God in Kabbalah.) The other inscription on the reverse side has various names of God from Kabbalah on it, but it is written in very corrupted Hebrew (possibly copied directly from grimoires that were popular at the time).

The rest of the hilt and blade is engraved with various depictions of Christian mythology such as animal symbols of the 'Four Evangelists' (the disciples of Jesus whose named are used in the Gospels of Matthew, Mark, Luke and John). and 'The Holy Lamb' which represents Jesus Christ.

The sword and its esoteric construction is a very interesting historical artifact because many of the Polish kings were known to be interested in the occultic arts. Ladislaus the Varnian wrote a manuscript on crystalomancy which is persevied in the Bodleian library, and Sigmund August was well known to be a practioner of alchemy and ritual magic. During his life, Sigmund had the second largest library in Europe, and much of it was connected with the hermetic alchemy movement.

Some scholars believe Szczerbiec was probably made at the end of the 12th century, since the first recorded appearance of the sword was when it was used in 1320 for the coronation of Ladislaus the Short.

After the fall of the partitions of Poland in 1795, Szczerbiec was captured by the Prussians and taken to Berlin. It later wound up in Russia, who returned the sword to Poland in 1928 in accordance with the 'Treaty of Riga'. During World War II, the sword was evacuated from Poland to France, then in 1940 it was sent to Canada along with the gold deposits of the Polish banks. It finally returned to Poland in 1959.

Szczerbiec is an actual sword and is in the possession of the Wawel Royal Castle Museum in Krakow.

Sources:
Wikipedia contributors, "Szczerbiec," *Wikipedia, The Free Encyclopedia,*
http://en.wikipedia.org/w/index.php?title=Szczerbiec&oldid=107128495 (accessed February 20, 2007).

Rafal T. Prinke – "The Jagged Sword and Polish Rosicrucians" An article originally published in *Journal of Rosicrucian Studies*, 1 (1983), 8-13.

T

Taming Sari: is a very famous keris in Malay culture. It is the Malay equivalent of King Arthur's "Excalibur" and was supposedly owned by the legendary Malay warrior Hang Tuah. It is said to possess magical powers. The keris was a prize from the Javanese kingdom of Majapahit to Hang Tuah after he won a fight with a warrior named Taming Sari. The keris derives its name from the original owner.

According to legend, Hang Tuah, in the end, gave this Keris to Tun Mamat to be returned to Sultan Mahmud Shah when he failed to bring back the Princess from Gunung Ledang. The Sultan had sent him there to bring the mythical Princess back to Malacca to be his queen. Hang Tuah then disappeared and was never seen or heard of again.

Another version of the legend has it that Hang Tuah had thrown the keris into the river, saying that he would return when the keris re-appeared. This has led some to believe that the real Taming Sari has disappeared, like the legend of the sword Excalibur.

The Taming Sari is unique in that it is made of twenty-one different types of metal- supposedly metal leftover from the forging of the bolts of the holy Ka'aba. It was said that Taming Sari could do Hang Tuah's fighting for him - if Hang Tuah was menaced or in any danger, the keris would leap out of its sheath, fly through the air and attack the assailant. The whole of the *sampir* and *batang* are covered in gold leaf. The keris is classified as a *keris gabus* or *keris terapang*.

The kris still exists today and is part of the royal regalia of Sultan Azlan Shah, the Sultan of Perak, Malaysia.

<u>Tarnkappe:</u> Sigurd's magical cloak that made the wearer invisible. Sigurd acquired it from the dwarf Alberich in the Middle High German epic *Nibelungenlied*.

<u>Theseus, Sword of</u>: In Greek mythology, Ariadne, the daughter of King Minos, gave the hero Theseus a magical sword. The sword helped him slay the Minotaur of the Labyrinth.

<u>Thoth, Book of</u>: Any of the thousands of papyrus texts claimed to have been written by the Egyptian god Thoth himself. The Egyptians saved many texts, on an array of subjects, in libraries contained within temple complexes. As Thoth was the god of knowledge a number of these texts were stated to be his work.

A unique Book of Thoth containing powerful spells and knowledge was also mentioned in an Egyptian story dating to the Ptolemaic period, which was translated to English by Brian Brown in 1923. In the tale the book is said to have been buried with the Egyptian Prince Neferkaptah in Necropolis and was sought by Prince Setna Khamwas, the son of Rames II.

Sources:

Wisdom of the Egyptians, Brian Brown (1923)

Ancient Egyptian Literature, Volume III: The Late Period. Lichtheim, Miriam (2006) [1st. Pub. 1978]. ISBN 0-520-24844-9.

Thoth, Emerald Tablets of:
Also called the *Smaragdine Table,* or *Tabula Smaragdina,* this text is said to hold the secret to understanding prima materia and how to transmute it. The concise text was a popular summary of alchemical principles, wherein the secrets of the philosopher's stone were thought to have been described

In alchemy, Prima materia, materia prima or first matter, is the ubiquitous starting material required for the alchemical magnum opus and the creation of the Philosopher's Stone. It is the primitive formless base of all matter similar to chaos, the quintessence, or aether. Esoteric alchemists describe the prima materia using simile, and compare it to concepts like the anima mundi.

The original source of the *Emerald Tablet* is unknown. Although **Hermes Trismegistus** is the author named in the text, its first known appearance is in a book written in Arabic between the sixth and eighth centuries. The text was first translated into Latin in the twelfth century. Numerous translations, interpretations and commentaries followed.

In its several Western recensions, the *Tablet* became a mainstay of medieval and **Renaissance** alchemy. Commentaries and/or translations were published by, among others, Trithemius, Roger Bacon, Michael Maier, Aleister Crowley, Albertus Magnus, and Isaac Newton; A translation by Isaac Newton is found among his alchemical papers that are currently housed in King's College Library, Cambridge University

Thyrsus: Also known as the Sceptre of Dionysus. The symbol of the god Dionysus, a ferula staff tipped with a pine cone and entwined with ivy leaves.

It was believed that the spirit of Dionysus was invoked by the staff. Euripides wrote that honey dripped from the thyrsos staves that the Bacchic maenads carried. It was a sacred instrument at religious rituals and festivals involving the god.

Tonbogiri: A legendary spear forged by the Japanese swordsmith Masazane for the warlord Honda Tadakatsu.

The name of this spear means "Dragonfly Cutting Spear". The name stems from a legend surrounding the spear that says a dragonfly landed on its blade and was instantly sliced into two perfect pieces.

Trisula: (Trushula) The trident of Shiva, chief of the gods in Hindu myth and legend. The three points represent Shiva's three aspects: creator, destroyer and protector. The name is Sanskrit for 'three-spear'.

Tranchera: Also called 'Brandemarts'. The sword of Agricane. It means 'the trenchant'.

<u>Tizona</u>: The historical sword of the 11th century Spanish hero El Cid (Rodrigo Diaz de Vivar), it was originally the sword of a Moorish chief named Malik Bucar. Tizona means 'The Poker'.

"And my Cid won in this battle from King Yucef, his good sword Tizona, which is to say, the firebrand."

The sword is 103 cm long and weighs 1.1 kg and bears two inscriptions:

"I am La Tizona made in the year 1040"
"Hail Mary, full of grace. The Lord is with you."

El Cid later gave the sword to his daughter's husband as a marriage gift, but when the man had treated his daughter ill, El Cid took the sword back and gave it to his nephew Don Pedro Bermudez.

It was believed that Tizona had been forged in Cordoba, Spain but Damascus steel can be found in the blade. This implies a Middle Eastern origin.

Tizona is regarded as a national treasure in Spain, and the sword is currently in possession of the Army Museum (Museo del Ejercito) in Madrid, Spain.

Tizona, sword of El Cid

<u>Tyfring</u>: (Tirfing, Tervingi) A cursed sword that appears in a series of Nordic legends known as the Tyfring Cycle. The sword was described as possessing a golden hilt, would never miss a stroke, would never rust and would cut through stone and iron as easily as through clothes. Its blade was said to gleam like fire.

The sword appears in the Hervarar Saga, as well as the two Eddic poems "The Waking of Angantyr" and "The Battle of the Goths and Huns". The sword was forged at the bequest of Svafrlami, King of Gardariki, the grandson of Odin. The king had captured the dwarves Dvalin and Durin to force them to forge a powerful magic sword which they made, but in retaliation they placed three powerful curses on the weapon:

1. Every time Tyfring was drawn, it would need to kill a man before it could be re-sheathed.
2. Tyfring would be the cause of three great evils acts.

3. The sword would eventually kill Svafrlami himself.

The berserker Arngrim pillaged Gardariki and engaged King Svafrlami in combat. Tyfring cut through Arngrim's shield, but the warrior got hold of Tyfring and wretched it from the hands of the king, then cut him down with it. The third curse had taken effect.

Arngrim passed down the sword to his son Agantyr, but the curse of Tyfring ended up causing Agantyr and his eleven brothers to go beserk and kill each other. Tyfring was buried with their bodies, but Agantyr's daughter Hervor entered the burial mound and begged for dead father for the sword. Agantyr gave her Tyfring, but warned her that the cursed blade would bring as much sorrow as it did success in battle.

Hervor gave Tyfring to her son Heidrek, but Heidrek was ill-natured and violent. One day, when his brother Agantyr Hofundsson asked Heidrek to look at the sword, Heidrek began to unsheath it but the dwarven curse caused Heidrek to kill his brother in order to resheath it.

Later, Heidrek became a king but the last of the three evil acts occurred when Heidrek was betrayed by eight of his barons, who broke into his tent and slew him with Tyfring. But Heidrek's son, Agantyr Heidrekkson (named for his brother and grandfather) pursued the eight dukes, killed them and reclaimed the sword which now was no longer cursed.

Agantyr then used the sword in the 'Battle of the Goths and Huns'. Although the Huns greatly outnumbered the Goths, Agantyr evened the odds because of Tyfring's power, and the Goths won.

Sources:
Elder Edda, The Waking of Angantyr

Stora mytologiska uppslagsboken, Henrikson, Alf (1998)

V

Vajra, a thunderbolt of Indra, king of the gods. Similar to the Thunderbolts of Zeus (See 'Zeus, Thunderbolts of')

Valkyrie, spears of: The Valkryrie were said to have spears with flaming barbs.

Vorpal Blade: An invention of Lewis Carroll, the Vorpal Blade was first mentioned in the fictional fantasy story Through the Looking Glass, and What Alice Found There (1871).

In the story, Humpty Dumpty relates the poem 'Jabberwocky' to Alice about a dragon slayer who wielded a 'Vorpal Blade'.

> *"Twas brillig, and the slithy toves*
> *Did gyre and gimble in the wabe;*
> *All mimsy were the borogoves,*
> *And the mome raths outgrabe.*
> *'Beware the Jabberwock, my son!*
> *The jaws that bite, the claws that catch!*
> *Beware the Jubjub bird, and shun*
> *The frumious Bandersnatch!'*
> *He took his vorpal sword in hand:*
> *Long time the manxome foe he sought--*
> *So rested he by the Tumtum tree,*
> *And stood awhile in thought.*
> *And as in uffish thought he stood,*
> *The Jabberwock, with eyes of flame,*
> *Came whiffling through the tulgey wood,*

And burbled as it came!
One, two! One, two! And through and through
The vorpal blade went snicker-snack!
He left it dead, and with its head
He went galumphing back.
'And hast thou slain the Jabberwock?
Come to my arms, my beamish boy!
O frabjous day! Callooh! Callay!'
He chortled in his joy.
'Twas brillig, and the slithy toves
Did gyre and gimble in the wabe;
All mimsy were the borogoves,
And the mome raths outgrabe."

The word 'Vorpal' was nonsensical at the time, but has come into the English language to mean 'sharp' or 'very deadly'.

The young dragon slayer wields the Vorpal Blade against the Jabberwocky. Illustration by Sir John Tenniel (1820-1914).

Source:
Through the Looking Glass, and What Alice Found There, Lewis Carrol (1871)

W

Wask: (also spelled Waske) Sword of Iring.

Well of Mimir: See *Mímisbrunnr*

Welsung: (Belsung) The sword of Sintram and Dietlieb.

Source:
Schloss Runkelstein mural

Whetstone of Hrungnir: The weapon of Hrungnir, a frost giant from Norse mythology, who engaged Thor in a duel.

Source:
Encyclopedia of Mythology, Arthur Cotterell

Whitting: (Hviting) Magic sword of Holmang Bersi, enemy of Kormack Ogmundsson the Skald.

Source:
Kormack's Saga

William Wallace, Sword of: A sword believed to have belonged to Sir William Wallace (1270 C.E.– August 22, 1305 C.E.), a Scottish knight who led a resistance against the English occupation of Scotland in the late 13th century.
The quality of the metal used for the blade suggests that it may have been forged in Scotland, unlike

other swords of the period which were often Flemish or German in origin.

Little is known about the origins of Sir Williams sword for it carries no makers mark and is therefore difficult to date. We do know, however, that King James IV ordered the sword to be rehilted in 1505, so that it would be more fitting to Scotlands National Hero.

The sword was traditionally kept in Dunbarton castle until 1869 when, of course, it was more fittingly placed in the New National Wallace Monument

Y

<u>Yasakani no Magatama</u>: The most important magatama is the Yasakani no Magatama (八尺瓊曲玉, also 八坂瓊曲玉), which is part of the Imperial Regalia of Japan, added some time around the Heian period. The Yasakani no Magatama stands for *benevolence,* and is one of the three items used in the ceremony of imperial ascension. In Japanese mythology, the jewels, along with the mirror, were hung on the tree outside of Amaterasu's cave (where she had hidden) to lure her out. It is believed to be a necklace composed of jade magatama stones instead of a solitary gem as depicted in popular culture. It is believed to be enshrined in Kokyo, the Japanese Imperial Palace.

The consensus among Japanese archaeologists is that magatama originated in Jōmon Japan before spreading to the Asian continent through the Korean peninsula. It is notable that the earliest Korean prehistoric magatama date to the Early Mumun (post-850 BC) and are generally found in the southern part of peninsula in proximity to Japan. Charles Keally, an archaeologist who has conducted research on magatama, states:

"The magatama's origins are more controversial. These curved jewels of jadeite are common in Kofun Period burials, and they are common also in Korean sites of the same age. But magatama are found in

Yayoi sites, too, and unquestionable true magatama are reported also in Jomon sites in Tohoku as early as about 1000 B.C., long before true magatama appeared in Korea."

Yata no Kagami (八咫鏡 ?) is a sacred mirror that is part of the Imperial Regalia of Japan. It is said to be housed in Ise Shrine in Mie prefecture, Japan, although a lack of public access makes this difficult to verify. The Yata no Kagami represents "wisdom" or "honesty," depending on the source. Its name literally means, "The Eight Hand Mirror", likely a reference to its width.

In Japanese myth this mirror and the *Yasakani no magatama* were hung from a tree to lure out Amaterasu from a cave. They were given, with the sword Kusanagi, to Amaterasu's grandson, Ninigi-no-Mikoto, when he went to pacify Japan. From there the treasures passed into the hands of the Imperial House of Japan.

Yggdrasil: The World Tree of Norse mythology. The tree joins the multiple worlds, its roots in the underworld, the trunk on earth, and the branches in the heavens. Its leaves are the clouds in the sky.

It was considered an ash tree, and consequently shepherds used crooks made of ash, and even today ash is still preferred wood for making walking sticks. It was once common for Scottism midwives to feed newborn babies a drop of ash sap to protect them against withcraft.

Sources:

The Encyclopedia of Superstitions

Ysbaddadan's Javelins: A set of spears dipped in poisonous venom.

In the Welsh romance *Culhwch and Olwen,* Ysbaddaden the giant is the father of the beautiful Olwen. He is cursed to die when his daughter marries, so when Culhwch comes to court her, he is naturally perturbed. He tries to kill Culhwch a number of times but ends up getting more injured in the process than his aspiring son in law. He then gives Culhwch a series of extraordinarily difficult tasks, which Culhwch completes (at least to satisfaction) with the help of King Arthur and his men. When Culhwch returns, Ysbaddaden is beheaded by Culhwch's kinsman Goreu, whose family Ysbaddaden had mistreated severely in the past.

Ysbaddaden is described as a typical evil giant of Celtic storytelling, residing in a magic castle that seems to get farther away the closer one gets to it and requiring forks to hold open his eyes. He is one of the most typical and memorable of his type.

Z

Zeus, Thunderbolts of: given to him by the Cyclops in Greek mythology, or by Vulcan in the Roman mythology.

In Greek mythology, the thunderbolts were gifts to Zeus by the Cyclops for freeing them after Zeus defeated his father, Cronus, and became King of Olympia.

Sources:
Encyclopedia of Mythology Arthur Cotterrell

Zulfiqar: (Also Zulfigar, or Dhul'l-Fiqar) One of the swords of the Islamic prophet Muhammad and later his famous son-in-law, Ali ibn Abi Talib. It was a scimitar taken in the Battle of Badr by Muhammad, and then given to Ali later.

There are conflicting interpretations as to the meaning of the name: "cleaver of the spine", "the two-pronged one", or "double-edged one" are all popular interpretations; although "sharp distinction between right and wrong", "the one who distinguishes between right and wrong" or "trenchant" are also common. It is traditionally displayed as a scissor-like double bladed sword such as on Islamic flags. Middle Eastern weapons are commonly inscribed with a quote mentioning Zulfiqar and Middle Eastern swords are at times made with a split tip in reference to the weapon.

In the Muslim world, the sword is of equivalent importance to Britain's Excalibur, and the inscription "There is no hero except Ali, there is no sword except his sword Zulifiqar" was frequently written on new weapons. In the Islamic world the sword is regarded as a symbol of honor and knighthood.

***

FIN

You can find more books by Carey Martell at www.martellbooks.com

Made in the USA
Las Vegas, NV
05 February 2022